managing
BUSINESS
SUPPORT
SERVICES

250 Number of online backups you keep.

0 Number of restores from tape.

NetApp simplifies backup and recovery.

Simply better backup. Now you can automatically back up your open systems environment, as often as hourly, with NetApp. Disk-based, point-in-time Snapshot™ copies provide fast, reliable, incremental backup of all your business-critical data. And NetApp delivers an award-winning data protection solution, with specialised hardware, software, and services. For simplified backup and recovery, call 08000 71 81 91. **Or download a white paper now at** **www.netapp.com/fast/recovery** to see how simplicity equals speed with backup and recovery.

NetworkMagazine
PRODUCT OF THE YEAR 2003

NetApp®
The evolution of storage.™

managing
BUSINESS
SUPPORT
SERVICES

Collaborating to Compete

Third Edition

Consultant Editor: Jonathan Reuvid

Capgemini contributors:
Mike Constable   Elias Mazzawi
Sunil Parekh et al

GMB

This third edition first published in Great Britain in 2005 by GMB Publishing Limited.

Apart from any fair dealing for the purposes of research or private study, or criticism or review, as permitted under the Copyright, Designs and Patents Act, 1988, this publication may only be reproduced, stored or transmitted, in any form, or by any means, with the prior permission in writing of the publisher, or in the case of reprographic reproduction in accordance with the terms of licences issued by the Copyright Licensing Agency. Enquiries concerning reproduction outside those terms should be sent to the publishers at the undermentioned address:

GMB Publishers Ltd
120 Pentonville Road
London N1 9JN
UK
www.gmbpublishing.com

Distributed by Kogan Page Ltd
120 Pentonville Road
London N1 9JN
UK

22883 Quicksilver Drive
Sterling VA 20166-2012
USA

© GMB Publishing and Contributors 2005

ISBN 1-905050-11-9

British Library Cataloguing-in-Publication Data

A CIP record for this book is available from the British Library

---

Typeset by MintoGordon Publishing Services, Alyth, Perthshire
Printed and bound in Great Britain by Biddles Ltd, Kings Lynn, Norfolk

Contents

List of contributors

Linda Berry
Linda Berry is Outsourcing Risk Director for Capgemini and has over 20 years' experience in the IT services sector. Initially working in technical and sales roles, Linda built a thorough understanding of commercial issues from different perspectives, which she now applies to contract negotiation. Linda heads the company's outsourcing commercial team and is responsible for interface with the in-house legal team on contracts ranging from small extensions right through to the biggest global outsourcing contract of 2003 – the Inland Revenue.

Mike Constable
Since joining Capgemini, Mike has worked exclusively in outsourcing, primarily in offer development but also in outsourcing consulting services. Specialising in thought leadership and the development of outsourcing services, Mike has advanced go-to-market offers for global Business Process Outsourcing and Data Centre Services in Europe. Mike is now a Senior Consultant in Capgemini's UK outsourcing business.

Brian Dinning
Brian has managed major AM Centres in Bedford and London since joining Capgemini 11 years ago. He was a member of the team that established the Company's Y2K Transmillenium Services service offer and subsequently managed the Applications Renovation Centre. Later, as Business Unit Manager for Capgemini's outsourcing business in London and the southeast, Brian worked on many outsourcing bids. Currently heading up Outsourcing Bid Support, Brian is particularly involved in bids that have a Rightshore element.

Mike Dodsworth
Mike is a Senior HR Manager responsible for UK outsourcing transitions and has 15 years experience in Capgemini's outsourcing business. He is an expert in TUPE, the legislation protecting staff who transfer with outsourcing contracts, and is a leading practitioner in the successful integration of new employees into the company. With experience of over 250 outsourcing contracts of all shapes and sizes, Mike's implementation of best practice processes ensures clients benefit from smooth staff transition and continuity of service, whether transfers are from in-house departments or incumbent suppliers to new contracts with Capgemini.

Steve Gibbons

Steve has managed the transitions for several major outsourcing deals into Capgemini, across utilities, retail, telco and defence sectors. His experience has played a major role in the continuous improvement of the transition processes and procedures of the group. Steve is currently Transitions Director responsible for all Applications Management Service Transitions within the UK.

Tony Kelly

Tony has held management roles in Consulting, Technology and Outsourcing in his 10 years with Capgemini including: Manufacturing Consultancy; the start up of the company's SAP business; development of ERP service offers; management of the Package Based Solutions delivery team. He also designed and managed Capgemini's UK Alliance Programme and the Third Party Product Reseller business. Tony is currently Business Development Director in Capgemini's Global Business Process Outsourcing operation.

François Labesse

With an engineering background, François has held senior management roles in the Applications Management arena for more than 15 years. François joined Capgemini in 1993 when he designed, launched and led the company's first AM Service Centre in Paris. Following that, he spent five years in North America pioneering Capgemini's AM business. On his return to Paris, François was appointed to his current role as Capgemini's Applications Management Global Leader.

David Langford

David has more than 30 years experience in IT Services and 8 years with Capgemini. With a background in programme management, David has managed a large number of transformation programmes, from Consulting through to Outsourcing. For the past two years, David has been responsible for Capgemini's Rightshore programme, within Outsourcing Services, that involves the distribution of workload to the most cost effective delivery centres worldwide.

Elias Mazzawi

Elias Mazzawi joined Capgemini's consulting business from an IT-intensive customer service management role in the financial services industry. As a strategy consultant, he has delivered numerous assignments in business design, build, cost reduction, merger selection and post-merger integration. Within outsourcing, Elias is an Executive Consultant specialising in developing Capgemini's business in transformational outsourcing and utility computing.

Sunil Parekh

Sunil has held numerous customer facing delivery and business development roles in Technology and Outsourcing, accumulating a wide variety of experience in over 16 years with Capgemini. He designed and produced global service offers for Capgemini's Managed Network and Security business, including product-launching the world-class Global Network & Security Management Centre in London. More recently, Sunil has extended Capgemini's outsourcing service portfolio by designing and leading offers in Mobility and IP Telephony. Sunil is now a Senior Manager for Capgemini's UK outsourcing business.

Bob Scott

Since joining Capgemini through an outsourcing contract with British Coal, Bob has held numerous business development roles in consulting, sector and alliance management. As Global Director of e-business, he was a key player in the launch of some of the company's most successful and creative e-business and CRM initiatives. Currently a Vice President in Outsourcing Services, Bob is responsible for Marketing, Alliances and Analyst Relations.

Russ Wyatt

Russ joined Capgemini through an outsourcing contract with Granada Group. He has over 28 years experience in IT service provision, with the last 10 in business winning support for large procurements with blue chip companies. Russ now manages a transnational business winning team and one of his current responsibilities, as a Business Development Director in Outsourcing Services, is to coach the most effective and expedient methods of helping clients and Capgemini achieve successful and enduring benefits – the classic win-win position.

Part One

Strategic Options

Introduction

'Increasingly, in the next society's corporation, top management will, in fact, be the company. Everything else can be outsourced', observed *The Economist* when contemplating the corporation of the future. 'Will the corporation survive? Yes, after a fashion. Something akin to a corporation will have to co-ordinate the next society's economic resources. Legally and perhaps financially, it may even look much the same as today's corporation. But instead of there being a single model adopted by everyone, there will be a range of models to choose from.'

This is a radical view of changes that are taking place, but not a wholly unrealistic observation. The situation in which a company is defined only by its top management may never be reached, but there is no doubt that there is a movement in that direction.

Managing a company is an increasingly complex business. Gone are the days when it meant making a limited range of choices mainly around product and distribution channels – what to make, how to make it and how to reach customers.

Technology has changed that scenario. The new generation of enterprise application software enables companies to extend their business processes and collaborate on a real-time basis with business partners on both the demand and supply sides. Collaboration has become increasingly possible – and in some cases mandatory – in a much broader range of activities.

The trend towards outsourcing is also continuing. Products have long been manufactured and sourced externally, but the extent to which organisations are outsourcing is accelerating, enabled by significant leaps in technology and communications infrastructures. Companies can now outsource activities that were once considered to be the preserve of in-house operations.

Economists would say this is a good thing: companies should focus on what they are best at, as that is where they add value. In the long run, everyone benefits.

Statistics indicate that the commercial world believes outsourcing is a good thing. Outsourcing is growing rapidly as an industry and as a business model, covering a widening range of services and processes. The UK IT outsourcing market is seeing the fastest growth in Europe; an analysis of deals and industry reports indicates a compound annual growth rate of over 20 per cent over the last 10 years.

Globally, IT outsourcing is predicted to reach over €100 billion by 2005. More than 80 per cent of enterprises currently outsource a business or IT function and more than 80 per cent have outsourced a core IT or business function over the past five years. On a global basis, IT outsourcing now accounts for one-third of IT spending.[1]

The picture is similar in business process outsourcing. Globally, business process outsourcing (BPO) growth is forecast at a compound annual growth rate of 14.4 per cent and is expected to reach $234 billion by 2005. In the US, as many as 84 per cent of enterprises are outsourcing non-core business processes. This figure is set to grow as more companies look to take advantage of low-cost BPO vendor-shared service centres and offload a broader range of non-core business processes including human resources, finance and accounting and procurement.[2]

It is estimated that around one-fifth of FTSE 100 companies have large outsourcing contracts (worth over three per cent of their market capitalisation), and research shows that these companies often outperform their sector indices.[3]

In the context of collaboration, four key themes have emerged – industrialisation, mutualisation, automation and globalisation. They are becoming a bedrock for success, and companies are increasingly turning to outsourcing to leverage the benefits of these trends:

- *Industrialisation* is about delivering economies of scale and a critical mass of resources to ensure standardisation of developed processes.

---

[1] Worldwide IS Outsourcing Market Forecast and Analysis, 2000–2005, IDC.
[2] Business Process Outsourcing at the Crossroads, Gartner.
[3] Outsourcing in the FTSE 100, Compute Weekly and Morgan Chambers.

- *Mutualisation* delivers multi-skilled and cross-trained staff to achieve effective workforce utilisation, and the flexible use of scarce subject matter experts. This reduces the cost of delivery and improves staff motivation and satisfaction by allowing flexible career progression.

- *Automation* is the result of applying tools to drive productivity, to make sense of complexity, to reduce time to market and to improve the overall value delivered.

- *Globalisation* is a relentless theme requiring organisations to leverage best practice across the globe in terms of methods, tools and labour cost differentials.

To take advantage of these trends, collaboration is essential and access to skills and assets, rather than ownership, is the driver. Choosing when and how to collaborate is a key success factor and there is a broad range of models.

Partnerships are most frequently on the strategic agenda and effective governance of these relationships is a determinant of competitive success. The scope, nature and range of commercial partnerships is growing, and skills in this area are essential.

The issue is less about whether to outsource and more about what to outsource, why, where, when and how. The number of options is growing and so is the complexity.

New forms of outsourcing are emerging, increasingly focused on bundling skills in technology, transformation and outsourcing to target fundamental transformation. Outsourcers are offering deeper collaborative models with innovative and attractive commercial structures that can reduce the need for up-front investment and move fixed costs towards variable payment.

If success is about picking the right horse for the right course, the number of courses is increasing and the horses are becoming more sophisticated.

1.1

The Business Case for Outsourcing

Identifying the drivers behind outsourcing decisions

Why companies outsource is a well-researched topic and numerous surveys give a broad spectrum of answers. This is not surprising. Drivers vary by company situation, by the position within the company of the person considering outsourcing and by the activity that is being considered for outsourcing.

A survey conducted by Capgemini and IDC found that the top three reasons for outsourcing were to focus on core business, reduce costs, and adapt to market conditions (see Figure 1.1).

Certainly, cost is always a factor in the decision-making process. But when asked their reasons for outsourcing, assuming that cost is equal, executives responded differently. The top three reasons for outsourcing then became the ability to focus on core business, adaptability to market conditions and the ability to bring about a business transformation.

This result highlights the fact that outsourcing is increasingly viewed as an essential tool for implementing change in the business, irrespective of whether the change is large or small.

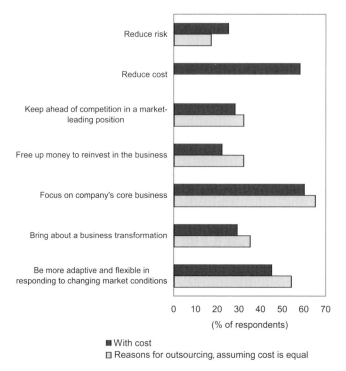

Figure 1.1 Drivers of outsourcing

In terms of what to outsource, themes include: outsourcing a well-run area, targeting cost savings and making a non-core activity out-of-house. Occasionally, and increasingly frequently, the focus is on an operationally problematic area with the aim of getting the problems fixed. Few are outsourcing a major area to achieve strategic transformation and accelerate the move towards speed, agility and flexibility.

The bottom line of many surveys is that there are three clusters of reasons driving the outsourcing decision – reducing cost, improving operational performance and developing capability.

The range of outsourcing arrangements has evolved to match these needs. The level of value created by outsourcing is significantly different in each case and the relationship and governance issues are substantially different (see Figure 1.2).

Traditional outsourcing is about doing the same task at lower cost, or doing it better for the same money. It is about sweating assets. The outsourcer achieves this through economies of scale, spreading resources and assets, and by applying best practice tools and processes.

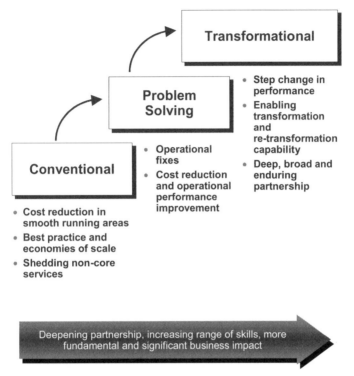

Figure 1.2 Key types of outsourcing

Typically non-core or 'chore' activities are outsourced, purely with cost reduction in mind. Justifying a cost-reduction outsourcing stance is easy when demonstrable savings can be illustrated.

The advent of offshore locations, benefiting from a low-cost, high-skilled labour force, has given greater scope for organisations to benefit from using outsourcing to reduce costs. But there are other initiatives being offered by outsourcers, such as grid computing and knowledge-rich helpdesks, that do offer other means to reduce costs.

Problem-solving outsourcing allows organisations to gain control, in terms of cost and operations, of certain troublesome business or IT functions. Typically, these solutions are considered for business areas that are unable to meet service demands satisfactorily, culminating in workload backlogs and potentially incurring unbudgeted spend, such as acquiring additional resources.

Justifying this outsourcing approach is usually a combination of tangible benefits, such as cost control and improved measurable service quality, and intangible benefits, such as customer satisfaction through stability of service.

Using niche players to effect a quick solution for problematic areas can bring short-term relief, but this may not be suitable in the long term. Consideration needs to be given to long-term needs as soon as stability has been achieved through outsourcing.

Transformational outsourcing offers the ability to use outsourcing to bring about a step-change in the organisation. It focuses on three main areas: technology, business and financial. The essence of transformational outsourcing is the strength of a wide-ranging outsourcing supplier that can take on existing services, implement new technology and business processes and bundle these initiatives into a commercially attractive package.

The headlines of the business case for such an approach are extremely compelling, particularly as the outsourcer bears a large element of the risk. However, it can be a difficult path to tread, particularly as the outsourcer is invited to become integrated into the fabric of the organisation. Nonetheless, the rewards are high for the business, as step change and agility are achievable, with many organisations then being able to leap-frog competitors and market expectation.

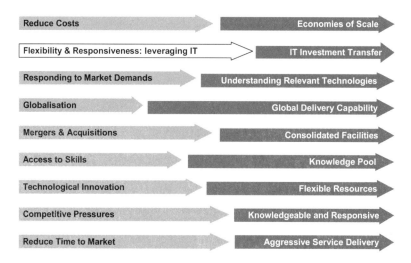

Figure 1.3 Outsourcing as an enabler

Businesses are facing continual change, and reducing cost is no longer the only reason to consider outsourcing. Instead, organisations can justify using outsourcing to relieve many pressures – speed, agility and product evolution to name but a few. Doing everything in-house might be comfortable, but it is not always effective or efficient. Outsourcing is an essential part of the corporate toolkit and used wisely can become a key facilitator and enabler for change (see Figure 1.3).

1.2

Outsourcing Evolution

From conventional cost reduction to fundamental change

After a decade or more of explosive growth, outsourcing is now a well-established business tool. Its usage is widening on two fronts: in the way it is used to achieve a broadening range of business goals and in the activities that are now being commonly outsourced. Gartner estimates that the number of enterprises that enter into new outsourcing relationships will increase by 30 per cent during 2004.[1]

Traditionally, outsourcing has been seen as a relatively straightforward cost reduction tool with a clearly defined and limited scope – something to be used to reduce the cost of non-core activities. Increasingly, however, outsourcing is now becoming regarded as a means of achieving a step change in performance. Transformational outsourcing – bundling technology, transformation skills and outsourcing into an attractive and affordable commercial package – is emerging as an approach to achieve substantial technological and organisational change. Indeed, IDC reported 79 per cent of outsourcing 'early adopters' agree that outsourcing is a way to transform their business, and

---

[1] Predictions for Outsourcing in 2004 (Gartner, December 2003).

over half of the large enterprises interviewed are seeking strategic relationships with outsourcers.[2]

This chapter looks at outsourcing's evolution towards the transformational and takes a detailed look at an IDC report that demonstrates how transformational outsourcing is helping companies achieve change.

Transformational outsourcing

Transformational outsourcing is about helping to achieve significant and affordable change by bundling technology, consulting and outsourcing into an affordable commercial package.

There are three reasons for its emergence:

- First, the need for change is becoming increasingly embedded into systems that are becoming ever more complex and inter-related. Many companies have their fingers on the pulses of their markets but cannot act responsively because their systems architectures and business processes are hard-wired to the past. For them, it is becoming less practical to outsource the current state for efficiency-driven cost reduction alone.

- Second, a new breed of outsourcer with skills in technology, operations and business transformation is emerging. They are able to combine that range of skills into a far reaching and lower risk approach to change.

- Third, change needs to be financed and the challenge is significant. Finding an economically attractive way to simultaneously improve short-term performance and deliver long-term change is perhaps the CEO's biggest dilemma, placing a strain on each organisation's structure, processes, technology and even its culture. Outsourcers are increasingly offering innovative financing models that can reduce the need for significant upfront investment and move fixed costs towards variable.

Where conventional outsourcing was about doing the same things but doing them better, faster and cheaper, transformational outsourcing is

---

[2] *Transformational Outsourcing, Helping Companies Adapt to a Volatile Future,* An IDC White Paper sponsored by Capgemini.

about helping to create a new business model and a new management approach. Where conventional outsourcing was contracted on the basis of long-term stability, transformational outsourcing is predicated on change (see Figure 1.4).

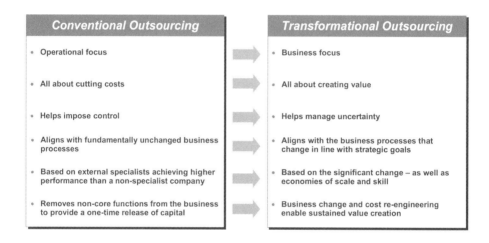

Figure 1.4 Transformational outsourcing

Successful transformational outsourcing depends on forging strong links between the boardroom, which is the source of strategic ideas and vision, and the systems and process functions that make the organisation tick. The collaborative relationship is closer, with more joint teams working together, deeper and broader across a wider range of issues and functions – and because of the nature of the commercial model, the contract is typically longer.

There are different flavours of transformational outsourcing. At one extreme is a conventional outsource with an allocated budget for limited scale change. At the other extreme, are closer and more integrated commercial partnerships, targeting for example, a specified percentage reduction in costs, but without a detailed roadmap.

Findings from a recent survey

The desire to use outsourcing to drive change is gaining currency. A recent study by the analysts IDC shows that outsourcing is increasingly being viewed by organisations as a strategic approach to achieving change and adaptability (see Figure 1.5). Companies operating in sectors that they consider to be volatile are around 25 per cent more likely to tend towards outsourcing; more than three quarters of companies are prepared to consider outsourcing as an approach to becoming more flexible and adaptable and more than two thirds of companies are prepared to consider using outsourcing to bring about business transformation. The full survey is attached as Appendix I at the end of this book.

- 79% of companies agree that outsourcing is a way to transform their business

- 70% are looking for an outsourcing provider that can help to enable their business strategies

- >50% are looking for a strategic relationship with their outsourcing partner

- 94% of companies operating in industries which they consider to be volatile, would look to outsourcing as a means of becoming more flexible and adaptive

- 83% of companies operating in volatile industries would look to outsourcing as an approach to bring about transformation (vs 68% average)

Figure 1.5 Findings from a recent IDC survey

Summary

Conventional outsourcing has delivered significant (short-term) cost reduction for many companies, typically in their support (rather than core) activities. But there is a clear ceiling to the level and nature of value that this conventional version of outsourcing can deliver. Transformational outsourcing can help accelerate and finance transformation, making outsourcing perhaps the most effective way of facilitating change rather than being just an approach to containing and cutting costs.

It is still valid to use outsourcing to do the same things cheaper, but it is no longer going to be enough competitively to rely on an outsourcer to increase efficiency (indeed it is difficult to find areas in which this is not routine). Increasingly, outsourcing is becoming a means of achieving a step-change in performance and agility.

For companies considering outsourcing some activities (or, indeed, even for those that are not), transformational outsourcing offers a different approach to transforming businesses and a different way to think about outsourcing. It is an evolving paradigm. The choice for management is the extent to which it chooses to embrace outsourcing as a means of facilitating change, rather than just a means of reducing cost.

1.3

Supporting Outsourced Services

Dispelling the myths surrounding automation of desktop support

A robust support strategy for outsourced services is critical for providing smooth running services. The difficulty is in providing one that avoids the need for extensive helpdesk facilities, as end-users require support on a regular basis. However, new thinking in this area suggests a way of providing support that resolves more incidents before they occur; empowers end-users to resolve simple issues more quickly than would be possible through assisted support; and reinforces the service desk concept to resolve more incidents at the time of logging the call. The aim is to provide more skills and empowerment throughout the support chain. This has been labelled 'Shift Left'.

This strategy can be applied to all types of outsourced service, but is perhaps best suited to those where there are greater numbers of end-users with similar requirements, such as distributed desktop services and business process outsourcing services.

A Shift Left strategy can improve the customer experience and deliver against cost reduction promises. The words Shift Left usually lead to an assumption that the service provider is trying to pull the wool over the eyes of a client by simply pushing the resolution of support incidents back into the user base – with a knock-on effect of making the user less productive.

The reason for this assumption is because with Shift Left, the goals or the process through which to achieve a successful strategy are not understood and expectations are not set correctly.

Shift Left is about increasing the user experience and increasing productivity, whilst reducing the overall cost of support. A robust Shift Left strategy will be successful when a balance between three value-based stages is achieved. Key elements in a successful strategy are: the service desk, self help and self heal.

An effective service desk ensures that incidents logged are resolved as early as possible in their lifecycle, thereby reducing costly and time-consuming assignments to second and third line support. The self help function provides targeted, easily accessible help and services – such as password reset to enhance the user experience – that reduces the duration of human intervention. Self heal describes the automated assistance requiring minimal human intervention by which incidents are resolved before (or as) they occur; the aim is to achieve resolution prior to user impact.

Human intervention equals cost, and the theory behind Shift Left is that support costs more the further it moves to the right of the support scale model (see Figure 1.6). This is due to many factors but primarily because of the amount of human intervention necessary to fix the incident as it moves to the right. Therefore, it is possible to reduce the cost of support by fixing the incident as early as possible in its lifecycle – by shifting the resolution to the left – where support resource is not so expensive. This is the principle behind the first value-based stage – the service desk. But the ultimate aim, of course, is to shift the resolution so far to the left that there is no need for human intervention at all.

The other dimension to Shift Left is the direct impact on the user. The further the incident moves to the right, the more downtime and there-fore loss in productivity the user is likely to experience. As a Shift Left strategy aims to fix the incident as early as possible in its lifecycle, this means that the user will experience less downtime and increased productivity where this is employed, yielding a much more positive user experience.

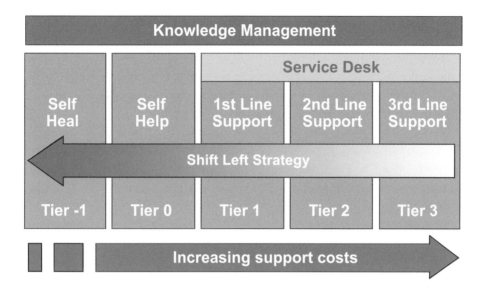

Figure 1.6 Reducing costs through a Shift Left model

Outsourcers support these theories by implementing Shift Left strategies in their service delivery centres. They develop repeatable processes based on experience, knowledge and industry standards. It ensures they are able to resolve more incidents as early as possible in incident lifecycle.

The area of a Shift Left strategy that usually causes the most controversy is that of self help (Tier 0 in Figure 1.6). In fact, the lack of understanding and misconceptions about self help can be held responsible for many of the myths surrounding a Shift Left strategy.

Primarily this is because there is a perception that the users themselves will be required to perform the support function. They will be required to help themselves by trawling through knowledge to resolve their incident. In its worst case, this is what implementing self help alone may provide. However a robust Shift Left strategy recognises that the more the user has to interact and take action, the less effective the strategy will be.

When considering self help, it is important to recognise at least three characteristics. First, there is more to self help than aimlessly searching knowledge bases. For example, password resets can be performed directly by users more quickly than calling the service desk. Self help is also a big step towards 24x7 support – an enhancement to the service outside the regular service desk hours.

Second, be aware that you only get out of self help what you put in – never underestimate the effort required to set up a self help system. Research shows that the knowledge must be context relevant and easy to access in order for it to be usable.

Third, understand that simply implementing self help is only a component of, not a full Shift Left strategy. However, when self help is implemented as part of an enhancement to the customer experience and not a replacement to the support service, then cost and productivity benefits can be gained.

The self heal principle takes a further stride to the left. Where the focus for the first two value-based stages was very much around making the people and process more efficient, this stage focuses more on the use of technology: how technology can be implemented along with process to move the diagnosis and resolution of incidents prior to user impact. This area has the most cost avoidance potential because it reduces the amount of human intervention. However, it is likely to have a longer return on investment because of the required investment in technology.

One scenario of this is where technology is used to proactively poll an anti-virus vendor's website. New patches are downloaded and distributed to protect against viruses that have not yet surfaced.

Another scenario may be where the configuration of a software package is monitored on a device; if anything changes from the original configuration, the software package is returned to the desired state. The user's productivity is uninterrupted and a support resource does not need to be deployed.

This is also the area that moves closest to the ultimate aim of shifting the resolution so far to the left that there is no need for human intervention at all. This is sometimes referred to as automated avoidance.

> *Self help* – this is probably the most controversial area of a Shift Left strategy. For this to be a success, it often relies on a culture shift within an organisation. It also relies on the setting of common goals, objectives and awareness sessions – these all help to avoid the common misconceptions.

A robust Shift Left strategy is achieved through the balance of the value-based stages – service desk, self help and self heal – as well as the financial considerations such as investment in technology.

There are some additional key learning points in adopting a Shift Left strategy: remember that although one solution doesn't fit all cases, it does pay to focus on the areas that offer the highest cost avoidance potential. At the same time, don't let the misconceptions of self help cloud the benefits to be gained from a Shift Left strategy. Be prepared for the cultural changes that a Shift Left strategy demands that can be supported by focused marketing and awareness campaigns, once they are recognised. Always ensure that self help is guided, easy to use and recognised as an enhancement wherever possible eg 24x7 availability, online services such as password resets. Finally, be sure to take the current service as the baseline in order to demonstrate benefits.

Understanding the components, the balance and the benefits of a Shift Left strategy all help towards dispelling the myth. It is clear that a Shift Left strategy really can improve the customer experience and deliver cost reduction when implemented correctly. As we have explored, each value-based stage is a building block. Addressing Shift Left at the service desk ensures better use of people, process and tools. It allows for support costs to be significantly reduced, whilst increasing the value of the service. However, it is still resource intensive and users are restricted to the agreed service hours and service levels.

Self help allows users to enhance their experience by providing access to support and services at any time without restrictions based on service levels or hours of service. However, whilst the experience is enhanced, the tangible cost savings through the implementation of self help will not be as great unless implemented with self heal. It is self heal that offers the greatest single opportunity for cost saving.

Managing Cost

Using outsourcing to achieve total cost management

In its early years, outsourcing was employed to manage the cost and effectiveness of business and IT, allowing performance to be measured against budget, and vice versa. The total cost of ownership (TCO) concept moved the cost equation on significantly. TCO provided a more far-reaching and rounded view of costs, looking at capital and running costs, support and shadow expenses within and beyond the IT department.

Today, there is an increasingly vociferous lobby claiming that the cost side tells only part of the story. Technology-enabled business processes, for example, allow more effective customer service, in turn encouraging customer retention and cross-selling. This can have a significant, sometimes overwhelming effect on the benefits case. It also proves that spot investment in IT can enable flexibility and that there is an 'option value' in the degrees of freedom this offers.

The use of outsourcing to manage IT and business process costs collaboratively has typically focused on cost minimisation. TCO addresses cost minimisation in a more holistic way and it is now a fundamental element of every enterprise review.

The game is moving on and TCO now needs to be supplemented with a fuller understanding of the value of IT that is equally understood by strategic business partners.

Outsourcing addresses the combined costs of TCO, by delivering greater cost management in three ways. In a traditional outsource relationship, TCO injects economies of scale and consolidation into direct and indirect expenditure, resulting in lower costs. In a problem-solving situation, the point fixes and incremental enhancements implicit in the deal avoid support and resolution costs, while also providing the benefits of traditional outsourcing. Transformational outsourcing moves the risk and cost of significant change to the outsourcer, putting on the pressure to deliver either reduced costs or greater cost efficiency.

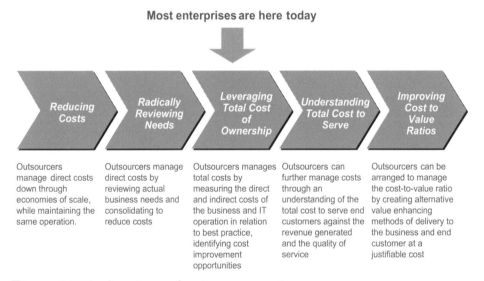

Figure 1.7 The five stages of cost management

Developing cost management

In the early days, IT and business process costs were largely considered as separate and stand-alone. They were focused on the operational costs and capital investments required to provide a service. This made for cost management that was largely detached from the enterprise as a whole. Outsourcing for cost management has since moved on considerably (see Figure 1.7), passing through different stages that each raise their own needs and concerns for the chief executive officer (CEO).

Outsourcing to manage TCO started out as a drive to reduce costs, but the activity tended to end up in a silo. For example, IT managers would focus only on direct IT costs, with business managers doing the same for operational costs. Any indirect reduction of costs was an unplanned and often unrecognised bonus.

One of the ways cost reduction was achieved was through economies of scale. By buying in bulk, the cost per capability unit was driven down. This covered all kinds of capabilities, from processing power and disk space to skills and human resources. From the outsourcing service providers' point of view, these economies of scale are delivered as a matter of course by buying capability in bulk and selling it on.

Outsourcing in this way is common practice for many CEOs seeking to reduce costs quickly. Handing over a costly and troublesome IT infrastructure to a supplier that can run it better and often cheaper is an obvious gain.

However, this simple cost reduction does not meaningfully consider the business value of the services provided, only the reduction of the costs for the same services.

Understanding what the business really needs and consolidating to further reduce costs is the next step.

The problem with outsourcing for simple cost reduction is that it maintains the same service, albeit at a lower cost. By default, there will be a built-in limit by how much the costs can be reduced. If there is no change in the provision of service, there will often be opportunity for significant savings, but they will not be radical.

The next step that outsourcers took was to review what a business actually needs to operate and strip out what is not used. For example, does a finance department really need the company's standard flow-chart software on every desktop? Perhaps the 'standard build' desktop exceeds the requirements for many parts of the business. By working with the enterprise to review the individual needs of the business, opportunities for providing a perfectly adequate bronze service in place of a gold service can be identified. Stripping out what is not used, or is not essential for everyday operation, reduces costs further.

Market analysts echo this effort in cost reduction in the approach taken to application portfolios. AMR Research in a 2003 report stated,

'Integration-savvy companies spend 11 per cent less on applications maintenance, services and headcount'.

Further cost improvement opportunities can be identified by understanding the direct and indirect costs of the IT operation in relation to best practice. This step was taken when it became clear that previous tactics were not meeting the challenges of total cost management. The concept of outsourcing for TCO management was born to address this failure and provide a more consolidated view of actual costs.

TCO can provide CEOs with a qualified view of total IT and business spend, as well as ownership costs. For example, a desktop service TCO audit will uncover both the direct and indirect costs of providing the service and how that compares to other similar-sized businesses. This, in turn, provides input to business cases for future IT investment.

At a high level, the direct and indirect costs are measured to provide a consolidated view of total costs that are meaningful in relation to best practice. This view enables the total cost of business processes and supporting the infrastructure to be reduced through services consolidation and reengineering programmes. This might involve harmonising similar services, such as back-office activities and the supporting IT, or moving to a lower cost-base.

The road ahead brings the enterprise as a whole into view for outsourcing and moves away from a blinkered view of costs contained in silos.

Understanding the total cost to serve an end-customer, against the revenue generated and the quality of service measured by customer satisfaction is the next step along the way.

The progression of outsourcing to manage TCO leads naturally into measuring direct and indirect costs in terms of business value. This is not as straightforward as TCO or the previous approaches to cost management. It has become complex because business cases for IT and business process investments are in themselves more involved today – cost savings and real business benefits are much harder to define.

It is important to have focus on the end-customer. Investments must be considered against the revenue generated by the customer and the quality of service or product experience. This is a fine balance to manage. Yet if the right balance is achieved, the customer will experience a quality product or service at a reasonable price, provided at a justifiable cost to the business. This does not necessarily mean the lowest cost to the business; the business value created might far outweigh the cost of providing it. By achieving the balance, business value is high because the customer returns to provide repeat business.

Outsourcing companies are increasingly delivering full business-service solutions and becoming strategic business partners. They can integrate industry and process expertise with a global technology and delivery framework to enable complete TCO transformation. Ultimately, transformational outsourcing is the mechanism propelling the wave to a total-cost-to-serve environment.

Managing the cost-to-value ratio down through alternative, but value-enhancing, methods of delivery to the business and end-customer at a justifiable cost is the final stage along the road to total cost management, and an extension of the total-cost-to-serve approach. By understanding the business value derived from the cost, revenue and quality balance, strategic business partners can manage total cost-to-value ratios for the business (see Figure 1.8).

When understanding the total cost-to-serve, the costs are just one aspect of the business value triangle.

The focus becomes enterprise-wide and begins to include the end customer. The goal shifts to a balance between a quality service or product at a good price delivered at a minimal cost.

Figure 1.8 The quality, cost and revenue challenge

The cost-to-value ratio is the ratio between the direct value to the business as a whole and the investment, including ongoing costs, in delivering part or all of a service or product. It is possible to be driving high business value through an understanding of total-cost-to-serve yet still have an opportunity for improved total-cost-to-value ratios. This sounds complex, and it is, but it can be broken down.

Considering a total-cost-to-value ratio for a whole business is daunting, making it logical to break the business into individual components that provide a service or product. Logical splits may be made between the front office, finance function, non-core back office and so on. The individual components can then be understood for the value they inject into delivering the customer experience and the costs associated with delivering them, thus determining the cost-to-value ratio. By driving cost-to-value ratios down throughout the business, a multiplier effect can be seen and the overall value of the business improves.

Focusing on cost-to-value ratios essentially drives the enterprise towards an adaptive operation that invests for the greater business value. Costs alone are no longer the key focus, and the size of the prize from changing the business, its infrastructure, people and processes moves into the spotlight.

TCO might be moving on, but total cost management is getting that much closer.

Where in the world?

Mapping a successful mix of outsourcing locations

Outsourcing to offshore locations is one of the fastest-growing sectors of the global economy. Research consultancy Gartner forecasts that 75 per cent of Europe's top 1,000 firms will at least consider offshore, defined as either nearshore or farshore – alternatives in the next two years.

A Gartner forecast also highlighted that the offshore business process outsourcing (BPO) market – including customer relationship management, finance and accounting, human resources and supply chain management – will represent 14 per cent of the total offshore market by 2007.

Given the means, enterprises will seek relentlessly to lower costs and become more efficient. As the advantage of an efficiency lever like offshore outsourcing increases, firms that lag behind will soon worry that they will ultimately become uncompetitive.

The labour cost advantages of farshore locations are well known, but this is only part of the story. Successful organisations are pursuing a strategy that mixes outsourcing locations for best results, rather than simply offshoring.

The offshore move started when companies shifted discrete, easily identifiable, project activities – such as applications development – to offshore providers. This is now a relatively mature market.

Selected support activities with real-time connections to the business, such as desktop and network support, were the next candidates for a move offshore. Now it is the turn of business processes, such as finance and accounting and customer relationship management, to be considered for outsourcing around the globe.

The decision to move activities offshore involves far more than simply searching out the lowest-cost location. Activities should be located where they function most efficiently and effectively with the right balance of cost, flexibility and risk (see Figure 1.9).

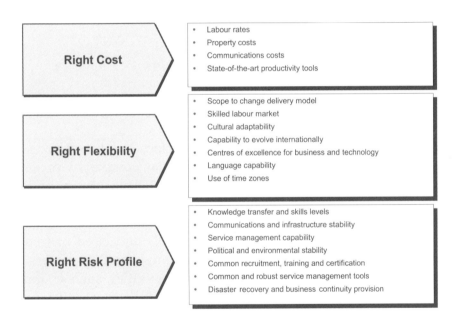

Figure 1.9 Three key principles underpin choice of location

This might mean locating some activities in a farshore environment, but more typically it will mean siting a blend of capabilities in various locations, be they onsite, onshore delivery within the same country, nearshore delivery from nearby countries, or farshore locations delivery from different continents. The mix must be tailored and co-ordinated to meet specific business goals (see Figure 1.10).

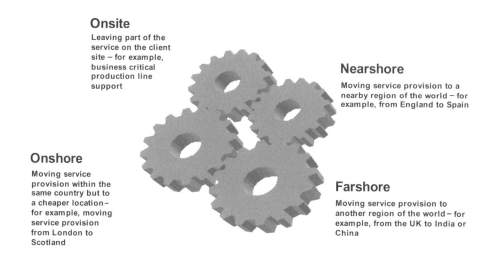

Onsite
Leaving part of the service on the client site – for example, business critical production line support

Nearshore
Moving service provision to a nearby region of the world – for example, from England to Spain

Onshore
Moving service provision within the same country but to a cheaper location – for example, moving service provision from London to Scotland

Farshore
Moving service provision to another region of the world – for example, from the UK to India or China

Figure 1.10 A global delivery portfolio

Making the right decision about where to locate delivery takes into account the best configuration for a particular company's processes, services and functions, making the most of labour arbitrage opportunities while ensuring the appropriate skills and services are provided from the most efficient locations.

If a support process demands unique skills and close or frequent customer contact, the best decision might be to keep that process, or a portion of it, onshore or even onsite. Other activities, such as applications or network management, might promise the most efficiency by being performed in countries close by nearshore sites. Similarly, to take full advantage of the available labour and site cost differentials, routine, standard processes are often prime candidates for farshore outsourcing. The key to success lies in making the right decision in each case.

The choice of location is clearly about more than lower labour costs alone. It focuses on efficiency through specialisation and economies of scale (see Figure 1.11). Global centres of excellence are key both to the value proposition and to delivery of results and economic benefits. Significant transformation is also involved, accelerated through access to best practice and state-of-the-art centres.

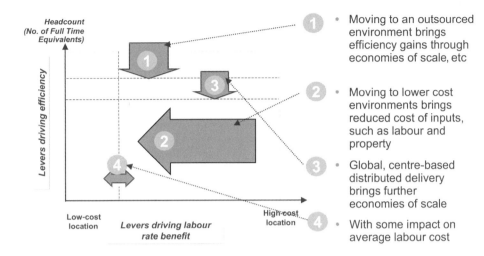

Figure 1.11 Specialisation and economies of scale

Emerging locations

India is the best-known farshore outsourcing location, but many other countries have a significant role to play. In August 2003, *Business Week* reported that while China supplies back-office support primarily to neighbouring Asian countries, its global reach is extending. According to *Business Week*, 'It is making inroads as an outsourcing base principally for English-speaking nations, a business dominated by India, because of the influx of western multinationals that are now bringing back-office work to China'.

Gartner predicts that by 2007, China will account for $27 billion in services, including call centre and back-office activities, reaching parity with India.

But China is not the only candidate. McKinsey & Co reports that Poland's services market is on the increase, stating, 'Poland's similarity to Western Europe makes it well positioned to become the BPO centre for Europe. If this happens, 200,000 new jobs could be created by 2008, even with highly conservative estimates of a 7 per cent share in the European market and a 1.5 per cent share in the US offshoring markets'.

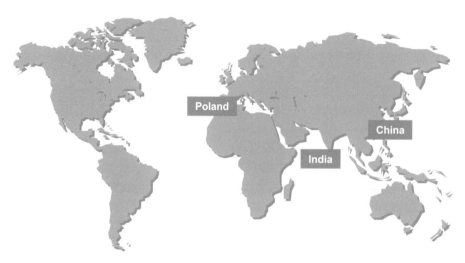

Figure 1.12 Leading delivery locations

Many companies opt to work collaboratively with a strategic partner that has extensive IT and BPO experience to help make and implement delivery location decisions. A single outsourcing partner that not only assists in making these decisions, but also makes sure they are implemented in a concerted way, has many advantages. Such a partnership enables productivity gains through access to best practice, scale economies, leading-edge technologies and top talent.

Capgemini's approach to combining onsite, onshore, nearshore and farshore is the Rightshore™ model. It is designed to produce results that work. Some of its key success factors lie in transition and operational excellence, such as an effective communications and knowledge infrastructure, high-quality governance and well-defined and managed service levels. The Rightshore™ model is also based on three other solid foundation stones: a single operating model; global support coupled with local service and effective knowledge transfer.

A single, world-class operating model, and a unified approach to service management is the glue that holds together an effective outsourcing portfolio. A strong standardisation programme, using quality standards such as the IT Infrastructure Library (ITIL) and Capability Maturity Model (CMM), can bring every delivery network component up to the same level of quality, consistency and reliability. Service centres should look and feel the same and operate in the same way, no matter where they are. Common management processes featuring uniform quality control and state-of-the-art productivity tools should be supported by standardised global training.

A global outsourcing model will have front-office and back-office components. Communication between client and supplier focuses on a front office that, in turn, connects with a back office that provides offsite support. The front office is the face-to-face, single point of contact and accountability between client and provider. It is in the client's locale and time zone, speaks the client's language and shares the client's business culture. When setting up a front office and back-office model, initial configurations should be expected to evolve as people become familiar with the Rightshore® concept. Within a year or so, the front office will have moved from a 'thick' to a 'thin' operation, with only the essential components of the front office located locally.

Under a Rightshore® strategy, significant staff transfers between the customer and the outsourcer are difficult, but retaining and transferring critical knowledge is essential. Where skills reside and whether they can be transferred effectively is a major factor in the onsite, onshore, nearshore, farshore decision. People with essential knowledge and expertise are usually retained in the front office.

The reality of Rightshore®

In an effort to cut costs, the European subsidiary of a global manufacturing company with 11,000 employees in 17 countries decided to outsource applications maintenance. The applications mix covered legacy enterprise resource planning systems and custom developed applications on a mainframe platform deployed across Belgium, France, Germany, Ireland, Italy, Sweden, Spain and the UK.

Discussions identified the major stumbling block: end-users needed local, in-country support in seven European languages. Despite some obvious cost savings, offshore service providers with limited language and business skills were clearly not the answer.

The problem was solved with a Rightshore® approach using both nearshore and farshore solutions. Nearshore, a team of consultants located in France and Germany can fly out at short notice to support critical show-stoppers and provides close support to end-users; while farshore, the main service delivery team is based in India.

The Myths of Outsourcing

Adding clarity and reality to market misconceptions

There are many views of the perceived benefits and concerns surrounding outsourcing, but not all are founded on direct experience and truth. Correcting the common misconceptions associated with outsourcing and allaying unqualified fears could bring considerable advantage to those afraid of 'abandoning all' to outsourcing.

Essentially outsourcing is about delivering lower-cost, better-quality services and flexibility that businesses would not otherwise be able to achieve. It can be a complex activity at times, but misconceptions belie its potential benefits.

The majority of misconceptions are linked to the different stages of the outsourcing lifecycle (see Figure 1.13).

Defining the outsourcing strategy

At the outset, outsourcing strategy has implications for all the other activities in the outsourcing lifecycle. It is normally a time of limited, high-level information, and a time when companies have the most searching questions. Until an understanding of business implications is reached, there will be few answers to these questions.

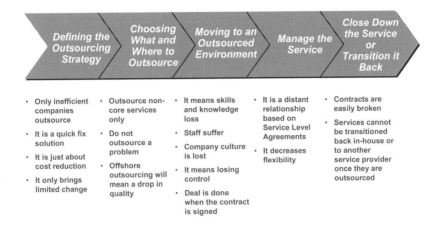

Figure 1.13 Matching misconceptions to the outsourcing lifecycle

There is a principle in economics that says companies should focus on what they are good at and this makes perfect sense. Companies have to focus on many business-critical, but non-core, and housekeeping activities on a continual basis, such as keeping IT services functioning, processing accounts and managing customer relationships. Following the economic principle, outsourcing allows businesses to do what they are best at by transferring non-core activities to outsourcing companies that specialise in delivering such services.

While few companies take this approach to the letter, there are many examples of efficient companies outsourcing key, non-core business services such as IT, finance and accounting, procurement and human resources.

The efficiencies of outsourcing

Dairyfarm, a fast moving consumer goods group in Asia Pacific, outsourced its finance and accounting services to Capgemini. This involved accounts for over 30 legal entities and delivered 40 per cent cost improvement through best practice and efficiency gains.

Corus, a leading global manufacturer of steel, outsourced the transformation of their IT operation to help the company reach its new business vision; the result was a 20 per cent saving on IT budget and IT services levels maintained at 99 per cent plus.

Outsourcing can be used either tactically to fill gaps and cut costs, or strategically to underpin greater business transformation. Where point solutions are the most appropriate, it can avoid the need for more drastic measures by lowering cost through efficiency improvements. Similarly businesses under organisational strain, with few resources or little time to implement new practices, can use outsourcing to achieve their aims quickly and effectively.

Outsourcing is almost always linked to reducing cost, and cost is a key lever, but is not the whole story in deciding the outcome. Outsourcing can enable strategic business goals by removing the need to focus on non-core activities and reduce organisational and technological strain. It provides access to world-class capabilities and technologies and access to volume flexibility, while giving management a sharper focus on core activities.

Traditionally, outsourcing has been about doing the same things, but better, cheaper and faster. The motivation has been cost reduction rather than paradigm change. But transformational outsourcing has changed all that, delivering a step change in an organisation's speed, agility and flexibility.

Transformational outsourcing combines consulting, technology and outsourcing to stimulate and facilitate business change. Where traditional outsourcing was about doing the same things, transformational outsourcing is about creating a new business model – a step-change in performance on the key dimensions of speed, agility and flexibility.

Choosing what and where to outsource

The decision of what to outsource and from where to deliver services is critical. Misconceptions in this area are typically born from bad experience or poor information. The complication is that the outsourcing industry is moving fast and its scope and network of delivery locations is continuing to develop. The key to avoiding misconceptions is to keep one eye on the business and the other on the outsourcing industry.

In terms of what to outsource, the argument that used to keep core business activities in-house is beginning to wear thin. Outsourcing used to be about transferring non-core, repeatable and technology-driven activities to better-equipped specialist service providers. But the line between what is core and non-core has blurred. Finance and account-ing, for example, used to be thought of as central to business and while it is a critical process, it is not normally what the business is selling.

If a specialist service provider can perform core business activities faster, for less money and improve quality along the way, this could be a valid option. Ultimately, what to outsource is a judgement based on the right outsourcer for the right service.

Once considered bad practice, today it is feasible to outsource problems. Conventional wisdom said only well-run operations should be outsourced and problems should be fixed in-house. The logic was based on the argument that it was too complex to use third parties to fix and run problems. That logic is misplaced, and outsourcers are geared up for and have many years' experience of problem-solving. By invest-ing in often expensive skilled resources, processes and tools, they can resolve problems for multiple clients by sharing the investments as necessary. Outsourcers also have substantial experience in rapid opera-tional performance improvement. Effectively leveraging an outsour-cer's core competence and investments can help to solve problems and achieve a shorter time to benefits.

Challenging the suggestion that maintaining service quality through outsourcing is difficult enough without having other cultures and methods involved, outsourcers are setting up operations in locations where there are high volumes of qualified and skilled graduates, very capable of delivering business and IT services. India, Poland and China are good examples. The fact that their costs are lower than those in the Western world should not cloud the issue of quality.

Additionally, governance and measurement frameworks monitor and manage the service delivery, and with commercial models based on risk and reward, services more often improve than remain static.

Moving to an outsourced environment

As theoretical decisions become practical activities, the move to an out-sourced environment involves transferring people, assets, knowledge and processes – all part of the enterprise. It is natural for concerns to arise about how smoothly the transfer will go and what the implications will be to the business. Here, management is key and any misconceptions need to be corrected before they create obstacles to success.

In taking on and delivering a service, outsourcers rely on staff, knowledge and processes to execute it effectively. Therefore it is not in the interests of the outsourcer to lose any of the skills or knowledge required to deliver the service. In many cases staff transfer with the services, retaining embedded skills and knowledge in the service. Additionally, where staff do not transfer, joint transition teams capture and document both processes and tacit knowledge as part of the transfer, embedding these into the outsourced environment.

Perceptions about the implications of outsourcing for employees are also close to many people's hearts and minds. Of course, some outsourcing arrangements require relocation or reduced staff levels and this must be managed sensitively, balancing the needs of all stakeholders in the context of external competitive pressures. More often, however, staff are transferred with the service, creating a positive effect.

For the employees, joining an outsourcing company can result in a broader choice of career paths with greater opportunities. In addition, there is business transfer legislation – in the UK it is Transfer of Undertakings and Protection of Employment (TUPE) – that protects the rights of employees who are transferred to another company as the result of an outsourcing deal.

In successful transition, culture is key. Changes mean an unsettling time and the more established the company considering outsourcing the greater the impact of cultural change. The bottom line is that culture is not lost, but evolved. In part, governance and the relationship between two companies drive culture. But many outsourcing companies' cultures are never static. As the companies grow through large influxes of staff following outsourcing contracts, new employees have a strong influence on ensuring that their new culture is reinvigorated on a regular basis.

Beyond people issues is the erroneous concern that outsourcing means losing control. The logic for this assertion goes something like this: 'If we own and manage all our assets and resources in-house, then we have the freedom to make whatever resource allocation decisions we want to target whatever outcomes we want'. This is true, but misses the bigger picture. Control is about governance and in this context the adage 'what gets measured, gets managed' is pivotal. Well-structured governance allows companies to influence the things that matter, chiefly business outcomes.

Typically, outsourcing relationships have tighter targets for outcomes than in-house operations, and measurement tends to be more rigorous. So, perhaps counter-intuitively, outsourcing can mean tightening control rather than losing it. In practice, for many organisations the freedom to make choices is limited by, for example, the availability of the right skills or too great a focus on fire-fighting. In contrast, an outsourcing relationship offers access to a wider pool of skills and resources, making choice real.

It is impossible to plan and contract for all eventualities in outsourcing, especially in long-term agreements. The contract is the start of a relationship and it is the relationship that drives success in outsourcing. The deal and the contract are about setting the framework of top-down, aligned and mutually beneficial goals within which the relationship operates. Experience of implementing and fine-tuning outsourcing arrangements suggests that success is generated more by the quality of the relationships than by the fine details of the contract.

Relationships of this nature need to be managed effectively with appropriate measures of success, clear procedures for addressing the unforeseen and effective governance structures and procedures. There needs to be built-in room for manoeuvre so that both parties can ensure the partnership is as appropriate to their circumstances and business imperatives at the end of year five as it was on day one.

Manage the service

After transition and go-live, the ongoing management of outsourced services initially creates a nervous tension. Services that have been managed and delivered in-house for many years are in the hands of an external party. The concern is that these services will be out of reach in terms of control and change.

This is not the case. Good outsourcing arrangements are based on partnerships and clear guiding principles that support the long-term goals of the business.

Service level agreements (SLAs) are one part of a good governance structure, designed to scope and agree on how services are delivered. They are not, however, a sufficient base for the ongoing management of services. As a business becomes more adaptive and volatile, the more flexibility it needs and the less critical SLAs become.

In essence, SLAs are a means of helping to control and manage the relationship between the client and supplier. They are not a substitute for the relationship and the misconception that regular interaction and involvement is not needed in light of some service agreements is potentially disastrous.

Indeed, regular interaction flies in the face of the notion that outsourcing decreases flexibility. The thinking behind the assertion goes like this: 'Once we outsource services to a tightly-defined delivery agreement, there is no scope for flexibility'. This argument bypasses the fact that outsourcing is about supporting business outcomes and highlights the fact that flexibility means different things to different organisations.

When the daily management of in-house services is about trying to maintain control and fire-fighting, the degree of flexibility is quite high. Resources, time and money can be directed to problem areas at will. In an outsourcing arrangement, that level of flexibility will indeed decrease, as the delivery of services and management of resources is performed externally.

By moving into a more efficient, effective and controlled outsourced environment, degrees of freedom actually increase. It is in the interests of service providers to find ways of removing recurring problems to deliver smooth services that are easily managed. It lowers their costs and enables the freedom to proactively forecast demand and be better prepared to deliver the right service at the right time.

This is a prerequisite to being able to adapt and change services. By providing a service delivery environment that can change with volatility, strategic flexibility increases and demand from new business initiatives can be met. The commercial framework with the service provider will be key in governing how quickly this can be achieved, but planning for strategic growth early in outsourcing commercial negotiations does help to create flexibility.

Close down the service or transition it back

Similarly, if a company wants to overhaul its service provision, perhaps as part of a strategic change, the perception is that this is not possible. Of course it is possible, just difficult.

Companies are rightly concerned about exit options and arrangements, and are often keen to ensure that early exit is an option. For this reason, contracts typically contain break clauses. Legally these clauses are enforceable but, in practice, breaking a contract is much more difficult, particularly if it is a large and complex relationship. Transition of the service, either back in-house or to another third party, is complex and involves upheaval, additional cost and risk.

Outsourcing is a long-term decision and breaking a contract is disruptive, making it imperative to invest in effective relationships that will make the right decisions upfront.

While transitioning services causes disruption and is unsettling for staff, outsourcing and then re-outsourcing (or taking services back in-house) is, at its simplest, a case of transitioning services twice.

The upside is that a lot of unknowns from the initial transition will have been overcome. Typically services are optimised during the outsourcing agreement, and moving them on again is easier. Knowledge that was not to hand the first time around will have been captured and documented, and bespoke applications may have been ported to standard enterprise architectures. Again, these will be more straightforward to transfer when moving to another similar environment. Processes will also have been made as efficient and effective as possible, making the second transition more straightforward.

The disruption of relocating people and assets will still be challenging. There are likely to be TUPE considerations and the trend to move services offshore may mean redundancies. The bottom line is that it can be done and businesses are not locked into a service provider.

New Technology

How outsourcing makes mobility and grid computing more accessible

Two key technology trends will drive significant change in outsourcing: the need to access systems and data through a wide range of mobile access devices; and the emergence of grid technology which is driving 'pay as you go' utility-based computing. Without outsourcing, the new technologies will stretch corporate resources and skills; many companies will look to outsourcers to become partners for change.

Mobility: new business freedom

Mobility is new and a rising part of the technology market. It is the ability to access business data and services regardless of location, time or device. Many people believe it to mean 'wireless' and the use of handheld technology. Although wireless networks and handheld units are key enabling technologies, mobility is a much wider concept, and includes all devices that have data to exchange. It is the equivalent of the internet for devices, in much the same way as the world wide web is an internet for data.

Key benefits of mobility include:

- the ability to share more information more often;

- reduced need to carry business data on mobile devices by allowing access to centralised data storage;

- ensuring data accessed remotely is the most current;

- more efficient use of time by avoiding the need to frequently return to base;

- improved scheduling of roaming workers through devices that share location data.

Mobility devices are not necessarily computing devices. They may be sensors or appliances with data to exchange, ranging from cars with global positioning systems (GPS) to internet-enabled fridges.

Conventional computing systems are hard-wired to each other in a predetermined manner. In contrast, mobile devices use wireless, infra-red, or other forms of over-the-air communication to make contact as and when circumstances dictate. A trigger for data transfer may include proximity to another device, its location or an event. Despite the motivation for wireless connectivity, conventional computers used as mobility devices may require additional hard-wired integration with other computers. In the short term it will not be a replacement for wired connectivity, but a significant extension of it.

Mobility solutions will be a challenge for IT departments required to support different makes and models of device, from personal digital assistants (PDAs), to smart-phones and wi-fi laptops, which connect and share data through a variety of channels. Connectivity can range from broadband and wireless access points, such as hotspots, to mobile phone technology, such as the General Packet Radio Service (GPRS). The short 12- to 18-month lifespan of PDAs and phones adds further to the support challenge of high technology refresh rates, training and support costs.

Providing remote assistance to users of mobility devices requires a support model that can accommodate a number of different devices. It will leverage a complex supporting infrastructure that integrates middleware and that requires enhanced security. For some organisations high service costs for a small proportion of mobile users will be prohibitive.

> A handheld device is used by a utilities service engineer to receive instructions to attend a machine breakdown on a specific site. It receives instructions from the existing conventional application managing engineers assignments. As the engineer is out and about, the information comes via a cellular call link. The handheld system also passes back information about the engineer's activities, such as time, invoicing and spares used.
>
> On reaching the site, an unmanned and automated sub-station, the handheld device recognises the location's wi-fi network and makes contact. It does this using security authentication for the engineer in conjunction with the enterprise network policy management. It allows the handheld to remotely access data files that relate to the equipment and procedures on the site, avoiding the need to both hold large amounts of data and manage updates on the device.
>
> High-speed communication links allow multi-media content to be accessed to enable the service engineer to be made instantly familiar with the site and equipment. Engineers without knowledge of the machine can respond as quickly as experienced staff.
>
> Stored on site are a number of spare machines that have radio frequency identification (RFID) tags to track their location, which is far more accurate than the theoretical tracking of manual asset management. The handheld RFID reader verifies their availability and records their use in association with the engineer to track who used them and when. The real-time accuracy inherent in this process automates the entire service, from internal event recording to re-ordering of spares. Spares might be held on consignment from the manufacturer and be automatically invoiced using the RFID data reader to forward the information directly.
>
> Scenarios like this one are also possible across a whole series of public, private and enterprise networks and systems.

Figure 1.14 An example of the potential of mobility

Much like the PC or laptop, mobility devices require end-to-end support, which is further complicated because the user could have the faulty device anywhere, at any time. An outsourcing mobility solution will aggregate costly and complex services across a number of clients and provide a single point of accountability. An outsourcer will manage all the necessary components, including a range of vendors, partners and internal or external support functions, to deliver a single mobility service (see Figure 1.15).

Utility computing: pay-as-you-go

Emerging virtualisation technology makes it possible for a pool of hardware components to be used as a single virtual resource. Utility and grid computing models deploy this technology, so that multiple infrastructures no longer need to be sized for peak loading. Spikes in demand can be shared over a wider asset pool, so that asset utilisation rates are significantly improved.

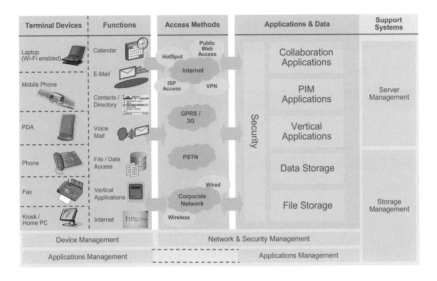

Figure 1.15 Managing mobility services requires an end-to-end capability

The technology relies on a 'virtualisation layer' to manage workload and understand and then reconfigure the available pool of hardware resources (see Figure 1.16). When resources are linked across a single organisation, this is an enterprise utility; resources linked across organisations use a partner utility; and a service grid is a utility that spans multiple organisations, much like an enterprise utility.

Enterprise and partner utility computing tend to use proprietary technology. Grid computing expands utility computing, using global standard technology to access a wider pool of computing resources.

The route to grid computing is straightforward in principle (figure 1.17). It begins with server consolidation, which creates more efficient use of servers in their current roles. It does this by consolidating similar workloads from multiple servers to fewer, better-utilised servers. It provides the foundation for smart clustering by having a good balance of workload and resource. The smart cluster manages allocated hardware within a limited range of servers, but it does not have the ability to configure hardware; its activity is limited to picking up spare cycles. Grid-enabled applications, which are becoming increasingly available, can then be implemented to share and manage resources across the enterprise, reconfiguring hardware as needed.

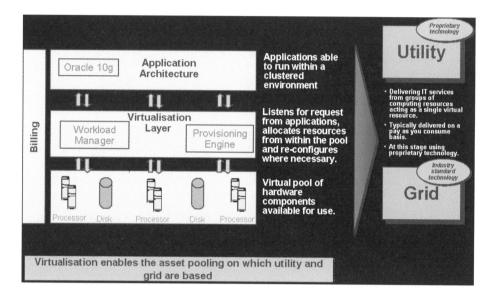

Figure 1.16 Virtualisation technology enables utility and grid computing

In practice moving to a utility or grid computing model requires significant transformation, overcoming technical and organisational barriers to reach the new world. As a result, it is likely that the IT asset owners of the future will be outsourcing partners who have the capacity to invest in building and running an enterprise utility or grid. Outsourcing will become increasingly about creating and selling on economies of scale, enabled by pooled resources, rather than about managing current IT infrastructure.

As utility computing and the new mobility technologies drive significant change, outsourcing providers will increasingly help their clients access systems and data through a variety of mobile access devices, and invest in grid technology to raise the potential for step-change reduction in operating costs. Outsourcing partnerships will become closer and deeper as outsourcing becomes less about managing the current state of technology they take on, and more about new operating models enabling flexibility.

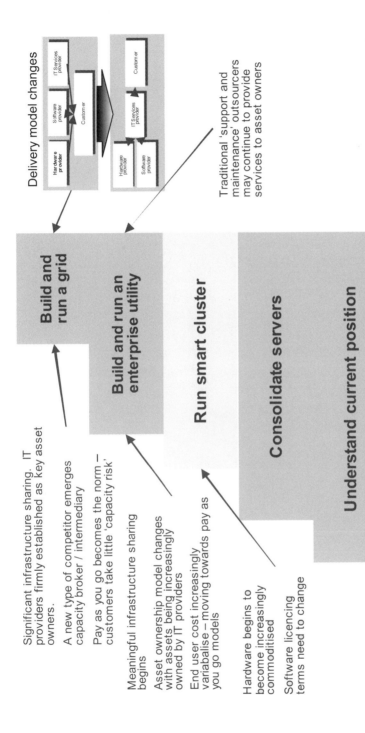

Delivery model changes

Significant infrastructure sharing. IT providers firmly established as key asset owners.

A new type of competitor emerges capacity broker / intermediary

Pay as you go becomes the norm – customers take little 'capacity risk'

Build and run a grid

Build and run an enterprise utility

Traditional 'support and maintenance' outsourcers may continue to provide services to asset owners

Meaningful infrastructure sharing begins

Asset ownership model changes with assets being increasingly owned by IT providers

End user cost increasingly variabalise – moving towards pay as you go models

Run smart cluster

Hardware begins to become increasingly commoditised

Software licencing terms need to change

Consolidate servers

Understand current position

Outsourcing becomes about creating and selling on economies of scale enabled by pooled resources rather than managing or transforming the as-is – assets will be increasingly commoditised, owned by the outsourcer and fixed cost risk will increasingly be held by the customer

Figure 1.17 Outsourcing will be fundamentally changed by utility and grid computing

Part Two

Good Practice in Outsourcing

Introduction

Choice in the outsourcing market has never been greater. Some suppliers have merged or disappeared, while new players continually appear, offering emerging technologies and leading business practices.

The survivors are those that succeed in the difficult task of balancing customer needs versus market dynamics. At the core of this sustainability is sensitivity and ingenuity – sensitivity to the desires of the clients' business and ingenuity to provide innovative and relevant services.

Based on Capgemini's expertise in outsourcing, this section of the book outlines the possibilities and potential of outsourcing, and provides insight into what to expect from each type of service. More specifically, it covers applications management, infrastructure management, security management and business process services. The concept of business fusion – combining business process outsourcing with IT outsourcing to create an end-to-end business solution – is also discussed.

2.1

Applications Management

Unlocking potential throughout a partnership approach

The clearest characteristic of the world's economy is uncertainty, with unpredictable change now considered a normal part of the business landscape. Solutions that can be scaled up or down are vital to provide organisations with the speed and flexibility that is needed to stay competitive in a more connected and unpredictable business environment. Still more, these conditions place even greater emphasis on attaining maximum value from application developments, (see Figure 2.1). Against this backdrop, organisations are looking for new and different applications management (AM) models – models that are flexible, business aligned and cost effective.

Applications management is no longer just about savings in efficiency and speed gained from outsourcing non-mission-critical activities. It is also focused on gaining benefits from creative partnerships with applications and infrastructure management specialists. These can help with critical decisions about applications and IT investment, as well as protect brand reputation that can be adversely impacted by technology failures in the increasingly complex connected business environment. Partnerships can also support organisations needing to work harder and those seeking to employ their capital more effectively, while growing levels of connectivity make it feasible to build up reliable, secure and continuously available external relationships with key partners.

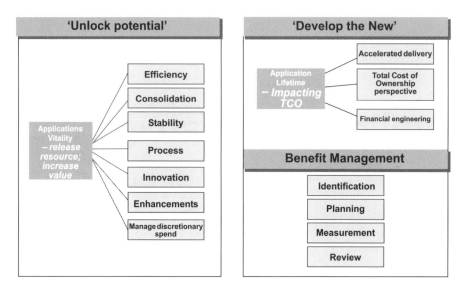

Figure 2.1 Applications Management can sustain business evolution

Applications management providers must offer products and services that recognise the value of investment in heritage applications and support the business and stability of these systems; delivering clear benefit to their clients' customers; evolving IT in response to changing market drivers; creating approaches that have positive business benefits on the total cost of ownership of applications. Providers must also offer innovation and flexibility in financing applications management, unlocking potential and supporting reinvestment into business IT development, while supporting variable service level agreements.

Organisations need applications management partners that cover these propositions and address key business drivers in a flexible way that can meet changing business needs.

Recognising the investment in, and value of, core business IT applications is critical and while stability of the applications is an imperative, this must be balanced with realising tangible cost reduction in their maintenance. The approach to managing applications must also allow for accelerated evolution within the confines of today's budgetary constraints. This is crucial to ensure that today's needs and tomorrow's aspirations can be addressed.

Research analysts have indicted that production support and enhancements can account for 95 per cent of the total spend of IT applications. Therefore, long-term savings can be achieved by working with an applications management partner in the short term to radically re-shape both the supportability of the applications as well as the means to efficiently support and enhance the applications. Best practice, methods and integrated delivery models all contribute to accelerated delivery and early realisation of benefits (see Figure 2.2).

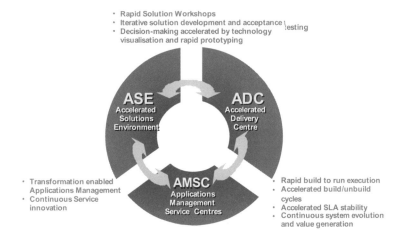

Figure 2.2 Accelerated business solutions – continual evolution

In terms of flexibility, carefully planned, reviewed and monitored service level agreements (SLAs) allow dynamic services to be provided. This unlocks the potential of applications management by releasing resources for reinvestment and maximising the discretionary spend available to the organisation.

This result is achieved by focusing on reducing the volume of support work, leveraging the investment in existing systems and prioritising development work according to true business benefits. Key areas that contribute to unlocking potential include improvements in knowledge management and sharing, improvements in resource utilisation and management, and increased productivity through request handling, problem fixes, design and builds, and deployment.

Organisations are recognising that the need for greater flexibility within their processes, people and IT applications is a necessity in order to transform themselves into adaptive enterprises. A suitable applications management partner can offer the depth and breadth of skills for a broader range of IT, and business process services provides organisations with the ability to use IT as an enabler for change.

Capgemini: the ideal partner

Capgemini ensures maximum benefit from managing an organisation's applications. Services include:

- AMHealthcheck – a rapid assessment of applications management organisation to measure its maturity and to produce a pragmatic roadmap for improvement;

- AMFitness – removing the headache of managing existing and new business systems via a low, fixed-cost base service with flexible additional services, according to business need, for a predictable price;

- AMVitality – maintaining business value from systems and reducing cost of ownership;

- AMLifetime – taking the long-term view for business continuity, adaptability and reduced total cost of ownership;

- ERP Run – full responsibility for ERP systems at scalable cost that is advantageous to the business.

All of these propositions are supported by flexibility of service levels, global delivery capability and Capgemini's accelerated delivery methods.

2.2

Data Centre Services

From server consolidation to utility and grid computing

Outsourced data centres' services are changing, as faster, standardised and ever more powerful technology is driving a revolution. Traditional approaches to outsourced data centre services are evolving to incorporate more utility-based pricing and computing resource, the implication being that services are becoming faster, more easily managed and can be purchased in ways more favourable to business needs. Achieving similar services in-house is becoming so complex and expensive that it is prohibitive for many companies.

Current trends are changing the shape of services further, with open source applications, predominantly Linux, and so-called grid computing delivering integrated computing resources. Ultimately, data centre services are moving towards an infinitely flexible, scalable and vendor-independent data centre of the future, driven by the need to reduce costs and match business goals.

Considerable savings can be achieved by outsourcing data centre services to leverage investment in vast computing resources and highly secure data management centres. Leading suppliers invest in state-of-the-art technology and facilities, offering economies of scale and best practice that are impossible to maintain for most enterprises. Buying data centre services enables cost to be driven out of operating margins and scalable and robust services to be delivered in support of continuous business services.

Over the past 30 years, data services outsourcing has been crystallising. Where it was previously about finding economies of scale and best practice, today the level of intimacy that the supplier has with the business and the type of services provided differentiates services.

Services are also changing to embrace advances in technology that link computing resources more effectively. It is now possible for computing power and storage to be offered in a similar way to domestic utilities. Such computing environments are known as utility computing, for applications that are managed across allocated resources on a defined number of systems, and, for the future, grid computing, which allocates computing resources across systems as and when required. Pay-as-you-grow, or utility pricing options, compliment this advance.

There are three typical ways of accessing data services and moving towards utility or grid computing environments. The first is by transferring management of an existing infrastructure to a data centre services provider. The provider assumes responsibility for a company's existing infrastructure and continues to run it either on the company site or by transferring it to one of its data centres. The service provider applies best practice to improve the level of service and allows the company to focus on core business. This route is most beneficial where a desired infrastructure has already been implemented but needs ongoing management.

This can be a first step towards utility computing, by initiating the external management of services and the application of best practice. It enables services to be more easily consolidated and transferred to the service provider's own infrastructure at a later date.

A second way of progressing access to data services is to transfer them to an optimised infrastructure. The service provider transfers a company's existing operations into its own optimised data centre and infrastructure, removing the capital cost of infrastructure, releasing cash and providing a more controlled environment to the business.

This method is particularly beneficial where scalable services and pay-as-you-go pricing are required. Enterprises benefit from a reduced IT cost per business transaction, advanced technology and skills, without the investment and adaptive scalability of the infrastructure.

This environment allows services to be transferred to an on-demand or utility computing environment, with automated storage, backup and recovery solutions. Outsourcing in this fashion is a precursor to moving to grid computing.

The third change involves creating bespoke solutions. The service provider and company work collaboratively to create a bespoke solution. This work shapes a unique service to fit the business and can be beneficial where existing enterprise or outsourcing provider services do not meet requirements. In this way, risk and reward can be shared across the design, build and run of the solution, exploiting the competitive advantage a custom-built solution provides. Bespoke solutions can also include multi-site delivery and resiliency.

By starting on a blank sheet of paper, the desired solution can be built. Existing data centre service components can be mixed and matched to meet requirements and new ones can be created – an ideal opportunity to create a utility or grid computing environment on which to base a cost-efficient and high-performance infrastructure.

The way that data centre services are managed is also evolving (see Figure 2.3). Traditionally, infrastructure would be managed from a command centre providing 24 hours a day, seven days a week operational monitoring services, first line support activities and problem escalation. This would be further supported by separate technical expertise in case of serious incidents.

The new approach to service management is based around an infrastructure management service centre. It is different in that all services necessary to support data centre services are centrally and remotely located, normally serving multiple data centres. The centre allows a dedicated team to support and manage segments of the data centre, such as groups of hosted services. Management is based on industry-leading best practices such as the IT Infrastructure Library (ITIL) to manage problems and changes.

The benefits are reduced cost to deliver services, as well as a reduction in both manual activity and costly out-of-hours support. Such a service centre also improves performance against service level agreements through service availability, first-time fix responses and a reduced number of problems.

Going forward, analysts and product strategists describe IT of the future in terms of being organic, adaptive and able to provide storage, processing tools and compute cycles on demand. In many visions, virtual data centres comprising one or many locations with the potential to cross organisational boundaries, support these concepts.

Linux

Linux is emerging as a forerunner in open source software. Implementations of Linux for internet, email and network services are showing significant cost savings -- as much as 80% – and although fairly new, its popularity is growing.

Low cost of ownership makes Linux appealing for data centre delivery. A licensing structure requires the software to be purchased only once from a certified distributor such as RedHat or SuSe. Linux is also platform agnostic, meaning it can run on a variety of hardware from the likes of IBM, HP, Intel or Sun. Platform independence allows it to interoperate with other operating systems, even when the reverse may not be true. It is based on Unix, and the huge number of developers and hardware vendors that support Linux are driving rapid maturity and reliability with their continuous contributions to development.

Linux is modular, so it is only ever as large as it needs to be. Linux can outperform other operating systems performing similar tasks in the efficiency stakes. The modular, clustering capabilities make Linux inherently scalable, a significant advantage for high throughput business services and grid computing implementations.

IT Infrastructure Library

Originally developed by the British government, the IT Infrastructure Library (ITIL) is a collection of best-practice guidelines designed to manage all facets of service support and delivery. It provides processes and an international language for managing incidents, problems and changes, plus methodologies for managing service capacity, costs and service levels.

Although ITIL has been prevalent for some years in first- and second-line support environments, it is beginning to make significant inroads into the management of data centres. While UK-born, it is also gathering significant interest throughout Europe, the US and beyond.

Autonomics

Autonomics allow greater simplification and automation of IT services by establishing a balance between what is managed manually and what can be managed by the system. The discipline is dependent on the underlying complexities of the heterogeneous IT infrastructure being hidden through virtualisation, using a middleware layer to create a single pool of computing resource that is allocated as necessary.

Autonomics delivers intelligent, open systems that manage complexity, measure utilisation and automatically tune themselves to meet demand. Systems can then adapt to unpredictable conditions and prevent or recover from failure.

Autonomics maximises the benefit and use of existing resources, while improving service delivery and availability. Tasks traditionally managed by a person can increasingly be managed by the system.

Figure 2.3 Trends in data centre development

For example, computational grids that allow the computing power for an application to be distributed across organisations are already possible. They are deployed today within academic and research institutions and are emerging in corporations, most often where there are requirements for repeatable, computing-intensive processes.

There is a clear roadmap for corporations that want to reach an adaptive state through grid computing. It has four stages, each building up to create greater degrees of value, connectivity and flexibility (see Figure 2.4)

- Stage 1. Server consolidation addresses a proliferation of servers, directly attached storage and networked printers across the infrastructure.

- Stage 2. Smart cluster builds on server consolidation activities to create clusters of servers that manage the allocation of defined computing resources through the applications.

- Stage 3. Utility computing extends the smart cluster concept with a utility computing device able to run any computing program on behalf of any user, thereby reducing the numbers of computers needed to service increasing demand for IT.

- Stage 4. Grid computing is the future, evolving computing model based on ubiquitous connectivity and allocation of computer resources both internally and externally. Although there are still challenges to be addressed when deploying these technologies in commercial enterprise-wide environments, there is a strong development focus and there are product roadmaps from leading vendors such as Sun, IBM, HP, Microsoft and Intel. These suggest that the visions will be realised in a three-year timeframe, supported by independent software vendors that are grid-enabling their software.

This will culminate in a data capture that will be always on, infinitely flexible, scalable and powerful, resilient and vendor independent. The changes needed to make this possible will be down to a combination of automated service metering and billing, virtualisation of processing and storage for multi-vendor environments, self-optimising and self-maintaining infrastructures running 'what-if' algorithms to manage capacity effectively, and security that embraces enterprise-wide identity management single sign-on.

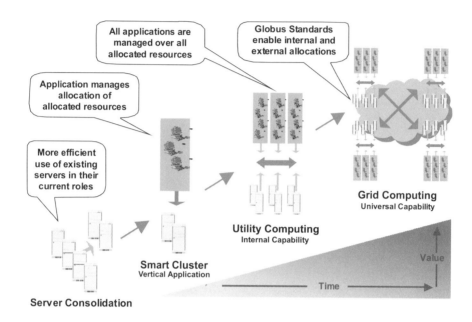

Figure 2.4 From server consolidation to grid computing

The ensuing benefits will be significant higher levels of service and availability through greater levels of management and efficiency, plus lower total cost of ownership through managing fewer consolidated assets and greater automation requiring significantly less human intervention.

Distributed and Desktop Services

Challenging the complexity of the desktop dilemma

Conducting business without a personal computer (PC) seems an impossible scenario. Yet the very success of the PC is becoming a problem for many organisations. So essential has the PC become that user demand for support threatens to overwhelm in-house facilities, placing greater pressure on IT budgets.

The pace of change is relentless in the end-user computing environment and businesses are now looking to capitalise on the availability of many access devices such as laptops, personal digital assistants (PDAs) and mobile phones to stimulate business growth and flexibility. The associated peripherals for the end-user computing environment have also evolved, with faxes, printers, scanners and photocopiers converging into cost-effective, multi-function devices.

Managing this diverse environment is becoming increasingly complex. This is further exacerbated by the overall IT governance factors that exist across the enterprise. Chief financial officers are seeking to balance the total cost of ownership against maintaining competitive advantage. Chief information officers have an equally difficult dilemma managing a variety of competing priorities, including improving service levels to end-users, reducing costs of their delivery and balancing innovations with legacy technologies. Additionally chief executive officers are looking for adaptability from the organisation, citing scalability and flexibility as fundamental IT requirements. The desktop environment is at the forefront of this need.

Cohesively managing this complex desktop environment has become more than just PC support, it has become a distributed support service that is a front-end business enabler.

A component-based approach for choice

Capgemini's InstincT service provides choices allowing the unique balance between risk and benefit to become a reality for all organisations. InstincT is based on a spirit of partnership, ensuring that business and IT work in harmony.

Choices become visible through a comprehensive component-based service covering service desk, servers, PCs, laptops, PDAs and the associated peripherals such as printers. The service is fully integrated and centralised with a lifecycle approach from procurement through to disposal (see Figure 2.5):

- **Procure** – The start of life for an asset. Covering purchasing or leasing through a network of Tier 1 suppliers and partners. Procurement can include the provision of an online catalogue for requisition, authorisation, ordering, receipt, delivery, returns and invoice management.

- **Install** – The asset is pre-built to the appropriate Standard Operating Environment (SOE) image, tested, delivered to the local site and installed by field staff to agreed service levels. Additional configuration and connectivity activity may take place at desk side or be managed through a remote tool set-up.

- **Manage** – Ensures that assets are available and that when there is a problem, it is resolved as efficiently as possible. Manage includes the provision of a service desk along with core processes of incident, problem and change management. SOE management, server monitoring and management and software distribution are all fundamental to efficient management of the support environment. eSupport is provided through a remote toolset, user self help (knowledge management) and automated self heal and resolution, and is where the benefits of Shift Left start to be realised. In addition, healthchecks, benchmarking and reporting are all part of Manage.

- **Move** – All installs, moves, additions and changes (IMACs) to assets are co-ordinated and managed through standard processes. Remote tools are used where practical to deliver IMACs. This will include key activities such as remote deployment of applications, user profiles and technology refresh.

- **Dispose** – Covering end of life and asset disposal services. Seamlessly integrated solutions designed to fulfil the total management of redundant IT assets. We use best practice processes covering collection, audit, testing, data wiping, repair, lease return, environmental disposal, product sales and reporting. This minimises exposure to end of lease charges, recovering potential revenue by re-marketing, ensuring data integrity as well as environmentally responsible disposal.

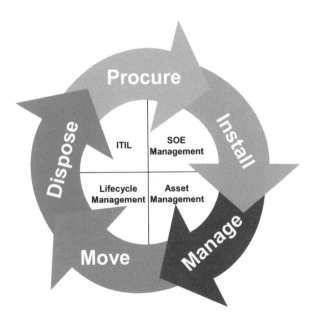

Figure 2.5 The InstincT lifecycle

Sitting at the core of the lifecycle are:

- **SOE Management** – A Standard Operating Environment (SOE) achieves a minimum set of standard machine builds, which are consistent and cost effective to support. Through a transformation project SOEs can be defined, designed, developed and deployed. Managing the SOEs includes maintenance via releases, fixes and patches as well as updating the SOE to a new base when appropriate.

- **Asset Management** – Choose one or all of the Asset Management services ranging from automated inventory collection, full financial asset management or even investment management. We can ensure your IT assets are monitored, managed and continue to provide maximum business benefit throughout their lifecycle. This may even include choosing to extend the life of an asset if it is cost-effective to do so. Asset Management, as a whole, covers hardware, software licensing, leasing, capital expenditure control, contracts, warranties, maintenance, software compliance, cost centres, procurement, invoicing and reporting. This provides key base data for making asset cost management decisions as well as driving down TCO.

- **Lifecycle Management** – An extension to the asset management function and completing the lifecycle of an asset. Comprises all or part of:
  - purchasing/leasing of equipment;
  - cascading – refurbishment/resale (including company/charity schemes);
  - disposal – safe and secure including data cleaning;
  - investment management – sweating assets, refresh strategy;
  - provision of a catalogue front end empowering users to purchase standard items within their agreed authority limits;
  - links to suppliers for fulfilment of order.

- **ITIL** – Service management and delivery processes are built from years of knowledge and experience and also using the IT Infrastructure Library (ITIL) framework for guidance. These processes ensure that best practice is observed at all times.

Simple, effective and innovative solutions

Many of the delivery techniques used may seem simple, but the simplicity of the strategic insight belies the planning and technologies that lie beneath. For example, the Capgemini Shift Left strategy seeks to resolve problems as early as possible in their lifecycle by building up the effectiveness of the early support tiers, where problems can be solved at lower cost. To this end, InstincT is supported by robust tools, including a knowledge management system that allows intuitive diagnosis of problems and thus efficient re-use of knowledge.

Web-based self help is also offered as an alternative to contacting the service desk, empowering users to find their own solutions to common problems and requests. The more users learn about their end-devices, the greater their ability to use them to their fullest potential.

Similarly, self heal allows users' problems to be fixed automatically, with applications protected and, if they change unexpectedly, returned to their original state. Users can receive help based on the action they have already taken, with options to fix automatically or solve step by step.

So convinced are Capgemini of the effectiveness of this approach, that costs to the client are lowered, leaving Capgemini with risk of higher costs if too many incidents escalate up the support tiers. Shift Left reduces costs for our clients, improves the productivity of PC users, and sets InstincT apart from the competition.

The future is closer than you think

The PC has played a huge part in making businesses work more effectively and efficiently. This is because it empowers users through a common platform to access the information they need and then act upon it. But today it's much more about accessing the information at any point in time, regardless of location. The PC will, in time, seem an enormously heavy piece of metal, glass and plastic with limited functionality.

Until now, business has viewed mobile computing as an add-on to their existing networked computer system, rather than as an integrated part. With business applications now becoming widely available for mobile devices, demand is set to explode.

Through its alliance partners and relationships with market analysts and technologists, Capgemini is forging ahead in developing our mobile support and delivery models for the future.

A world where the service desk as we know it today will no longer exist can also be envisaged. As Shift Left is adopted and the remote capabilities of support teams are enhanced, users will be able to perform their role independent of time or geography.

Capgemini is confident that it has a service capable of sustaining the needs of the user today; however the Capgemini InstincT vision evolves this service to continually meet the changing needs of the business.

2.4

Networks

Getting the best from network services

Organisations face two primary challenges – how to transact business efficiently *and* remain in a perpetual state of readiness to change. With these challenges in mind, connectivity and collaboration have become vital business enablers, making the management of the underlying network infrastructure critical to the business. For some organisations, managing network services is proving challenging on many fronts – technically, operationally and financially. Outsourcing offers an answer, providing a managed network service that introduces a flexible, cost-effective and relevant solution to maintaining current and future connectivity needs.

Electronic communications enable organisations to use both internal and external business processes to achieve competitive advantage, or at least keep up with their market sector, by working smarter and more efficiently. But as the pace of change increases, greater demands are placed on organisations to transact business cost-effectively.

For many organisations, the need to operate at optimum capacity and rapidly embrace change is often entwined with complex business and technical challenges, particularly for those trying to trade globally around the clock. Central to these challenges is ensuring that

both current and future connectivity needs can be fulfilled by
network services, while still satisfying the desire to reduce costs,
maximise the benefit of expenditure and minimise business risk.
Properly managed, the network can itself become a valuable business
accelerator.

But all too often the network is viewed merely as a means to an end,
its purpose to connect locations together, giving employees a way to
access applications hosted at remote data centres and allowing departments to send and receive information internally, as well as from
partners, suppliers and customers.

Typically, business units see managing the network as a back-room
function requiring specialist expertise that can be expensive to recruit
and retain. So the network is managed tactically, on a day-to-day basis,
with little thought given to the overall business vision.

When there is a problem with IT, the network is usually cited as one of
the main causes, especially if response times are slow or links fail at
crucial times. Often helpdesks cannot tell frustrated users the real cause
of the problem and, more importantly, when resumption of normal
services can be expected.

But when problems arise, is the real issue the network or the
approach to the network? One answer is that the business should
expect and demand more from the network, viewing it as an accelerator
rather than an inhibitor (see Figure 2.6). Ultimately, the network service
should be like any other utility – plug it in, turn it on, and use it.

Effective network services:

- *Readily and rapidly respond to change, knowing network services will cope*
- *Achieve maximum value from investment in bandwidth, devices and operations*
- *Restructure the cost base to provide flexibility and advantage to the business*
- *Simplify approach to interacting with numerous third-party suppliers*
- *Appropriately resource network activities with suitably qualified personnel*
- *Embrace and realise true business benefits from new technologies*
- *Successfully manage the impact of shortening vendor product lifecycles.*

Figure 2.6 Key features of a business-enabling network service

This can sometimes be achieved by outsourcing network services, delivering a wide range of benefits that touch many parts of the organisation from IT operations through to financial.

Capgemini seeks to develop tailor-made managed network services that address the business needs of each client. There are three broad categories of service – base, enhanced and advanced – that can be mapped onto high-level business drivers, allowing support for a stable efficient operation, right through to delivery of strategic objectives through leverage of network services (see Figure 2.7).

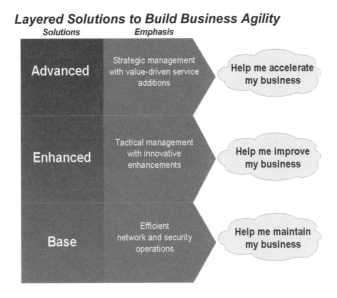

Figure 2.7 Capgemini's view on outsourcing network service

Each category is created by combining one or more service building blocks that allow solutions to be tailored. In turn, each of these has many service elements that can be included, excluded or refined as required.

Intertwined through all three categories are optional optimisation services, a range of discrete services that can be introduced at any time during the managed network service (see Figure 2.8).

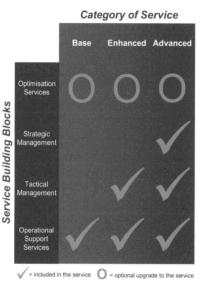

- *Management of network services is driven by the needs of the business*
- *Single point of accountability for the network*
- *Increased flexibility to embrace business change*
- *Cost basis engineered for business advantage*
- *Improved cost management, ability to quantify and optimise value of service*
- *Reduced investment for managing new technologies*
- *Increased service quality through application of best practice and carrier strength tools*
- *Timely and relevant service reporting*
- *Vendor alliances provide stronger links for support and strategy*
- *Supplier selection enables best-of-fit products*
- *Access to a range of qualified and specialised personnel*
- *Leverage lessons learned through people who have done it before.*

Figure 2.8 The benefits of outsourcing network services

Security

Transforming a business defender into an enabler

Many organisations face the challenge of working more efficiently and cost effectively with partners, suppliers and customers. To achieve further competitive advantage, with the overall aim of increasing value to the customer, there is escalating pressure to expand data accessibility and usability. But, greater openness brings greater risks. Further, the sophistication of electronic attacks, and increasingly complex computing environments, only serve to exacerbate the risks.

All organisations share the fact that they have security risks, but that is where the similarity ends as the level of severity and business impact will always differ.

The ability to identify and manage these risks, with appropriate detection and counter-actions, can be vital to an organisation's position and reputation in the market. Traditionally, mitigating these risks has been achieved by reactively deploying a security solution. This usually happens because of technological needs and the solution is often supported as a supplementary computing service. While this provides a level of protection, it does not offer organisations the full potential of using security as a business enabler rather than purely as a defender.

When considering how to manage security, it is imperative to have the right balance between the value of the information assets and the level of protection that is required to manage the risk of those assets being compromised.

Without adequate security in place the impact of a breach could affect many parts in and around an organisation (see Figure 2.9). This may include disruption to internal business operations as well as loss of trust and trade from customers and suppliers.

Figure 2.9 The impact of a security breach

Business-risk driven process

There is no universal solution to managing security. Our approach is to follow a simple three-stage process to jointly define the right service for the business taking into account the corporate policy for managing risk (see Figure 2.10):

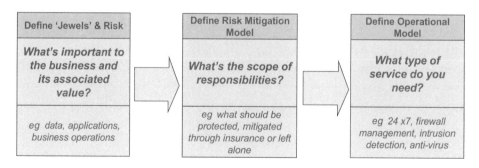

Figure 2.10 Defining a risk-based solution

- *Define 'jewels' and risk* – Initially we will gain an understanding of the key assets or 'jewels' of an organisation, their value to the business and associated potential security risks.

- *Define risk mitigation model* – Secondly, we will agree the approach to mitigating the risk for those key assets. Usually, this takes the form of protection through a security solution. However, depending on the value of an asset and the business's attitude to risk, options such as covering the risk via insurance or accepting the risk (ie 'do nothing') may be appropriate.

- *Define operational model* – Finally, for those assets requiring protection, Capgemini will define a specific operational model for a Managed Security Service based on the agreed responsibilities.

Successful ongoing operations

Deploying a security solution is only the start; the challenge faced by many organisations is keeping their solution operating optimally. This primarily means ensuring that the security solution continually provides the required level of service to protect and advance the business (see Figure 2.11).

Figure 2.11 A comprehensive and coherently managed service

Maintaining the integrity of the ongoing operation centres on three critical areas:

- responding to attacks and handling changes;
- keeping up-to-date with known breaches and vulnerabilities;
- continuing to protect the information assets.

Responding to attacks and handling changes

Security attacks can occur at any time in any day. They can range from minor access attempts through to major breaches where information may have been retrieved or destroyed. To manage such attacks strict process needs to be followed to neutralise the attempt and contain any impact.

Capgemini offers *event management* to rapidly identify, curtail and resolve every security attack in accordance with the corporate security policy. Strict control of changes ensures implementations conform to the policy (see Figure 2.12).

Service Element		Purpose		Benefit
Event Monitoring & Response	➲	Provide a rapid and highly responsive service for network security problems and changes	➲	Faster detection and resolution of problems using an advanced automated toolset, best practice and specialist security expertise
Detailed Diagnostic & Resolution	➲	Detailed analysis and resolution of problems escalated from the 1st/2nd resolution teams	➲	Rapid escalation and resolution of complex network security problems
Third Party Escalation & Management	➲	Escalation of problems to vendors/suppliers, including issue management to conclusion	➲	Single point of accountability for managing vendors/suppliers in line with Service Level Agreement
Problem & Change Management	➲	Rigorous control of all problems and changes actioned by all teams	➲	Strict control of all events under management by using a single source of information for an event, that is both auditable and re-usable via knowledge management

Figure 2.12 Service elements contained within Event Management

Keeping up-to-date with known breaches and vulnerabilities

As soon as an IT infrastructure is implemented, vulnerabilities may exist. This could be as a consequence of ongoing IT changes, continual evolution of technology or the discovery of new ways to compromise security. However, this raises serious concerns for all organisations, in terms of: How do you find out about these vulnerabilities? How do know that the vulnerabilities may be relevant to you? If they are, then what actions do you perform to close the vulnerabilities? Finally, what will be the impact of those actions on the rest of the IT infrastructure?

Capgemini offers *intelligence services* to proactively identify vulnerabilities and quickly action changes in accordance with the security policy (see Figure 2.13).

Service Element	Purpose	Benefit
Vulnerability Action Processing	Provide filtered and targeted intelligence on the latest vulnerabilities affecting client's IT infrastructure.	Maintains the integrity of the security solution by keeping the infrastructure in line with the latest security updates
Vulnerability Assessment	Provide non-intrusive audits of the network infrastructure including hosting devices (servers), firewalls, switches, routers.	Provides a cross-balancing check that ensures changes already implemented across the network do not compromise security
Security Review	Conduct a detailed review of the security solution and policy to ensure that the protection and detection is in line with the business priorities	Provides an independent and unbiased assessment of the network security, including steps required to maintain the level of protection required by the business

Figure 2.13 Service elements contained within Intelligence Services

Continuing to protect the information assets

Once a security policy has been defined and implemented, its validity can start to erode. This can be due to both external and internal factors. Common examples include evolving data access needs, changes to the underlying IT infrastructure and the emergence of new security industry practices. However, within all this change and evolution, the integrity of the network security must always be maintained at the level required by the business.

Capgemini offers *policy enforcement* to proactively ensure that the security policy is being followed and is also kept up to date. (see Figure 2.14)

Service Element		Purpose		Benefit
Security Officer	➲	Provide dedicated technical guidance and assistance for the delivery and development of the security service	➲	A single point of contact for all aspects of the security service
Policy Custodian	➲	Provide advice and guidance for amending the security policy in line with the latest best practice and trends	➲	Security policy is continually reviewed and kept up to date
Quality Assurance of Changes	➲	Review of all changes to ensure adherence to the security policy	➲	Integrity of security is not compromised by implementation of changes
Device Configuration & Maintenance	➲	Maintain software and hardware to current configuration levels needed to support the security policy	➲	Integrity of security is sustained by consistent and regular device maintenance
Service Reporting	➲	Create and supply timely reporting that is relevant to the service being provided	➲	Provides a summary of the service being supplied and assurance of conformance to security policy

Figure 2.14 Service elements contained within Policy enforcement

Defining the best solution for the business

To define the best solution for the needs of the business, Capgemini will combine elements of the three areas of Event Management, intelligence services, and policy enforcement into a single and comprehensive managed security service. The benefits of our service include:

- ability to manage security in accordance with measured business risks;

- single point of accountability for IT security operations;

- flexible solution that can easily scale up or down as required by the business;

- leveraging the experience and expertise of specialist security personnel;

- clear definition of scope-for-spend, ensuring the investment in security can be directly correlated to service provided;

- security becoming part of developing the business, rather than an exceptional addition.

2.6

Finance and Administration

A clear contender for business process outsourcing

According to research from IDC, 'Finance and accounting processes can be breeding grounds for inefficiency, laden with manual and redundant processes, priming them to be outsourced'.

The demand for real-time, accurate and transparent financial reporting to decision-makers, board members and shareholders alike is unprecedented. In the wake of 9/11, market debacles like WorldCom and the subsequent rush to financial restatements, executive accountability soared to new heights in the US with the passage of the Sarbanes-Oxley Act of 2002.

Challenged by an unsteady global economy, the pressure to deliver more shareholder value and intense scrutiny from inside and out, chief finance officers (CFOs) now bear the weight of increased accountability and liability. While back-office transaction processing may be fundamental and formulaic, the accuracy and timeliness of the information it delivers are the legs upon which today's executives stand to meet their responsibilities and mitigate personal and professional risk.

According to IDC, corporate collapses in the US highlighted the importance of a sound finance and accounting strategy. Mishandling of information can lead to significant losses for corporations.

The Sarbanes-Oxley legislation obliges management to 'assess and make representations about the effectiveness of the internal control structure and procedures'. This is of particular importance and applies to European companies that have operations registered in the US.

Certainly, survival in today's rapid-paced business environment depends on a company's ability to adapt to changing markets and competitive conditions. Similarly, the pressing need for finance units to contribute value at a more strategic level generates the requirement for timely and accurate financial information at lower cost.

According to research by CFO Research Services in collaboration with Capgemini, CFOs agree that 'too much of finance's time – 39 per cent on average – is still spent on transaction processing. Over the next three years, a large majority of CFOs are committed to using shared services or partial outsourcing to accomplish a reduction to 27 per cent of time allocated to transaction processing'.

In many corporations, changes in internal and external environments – perhaps mergers, acquisitions, divestitures, rightsizing, regulation – outpace process improvements and integration, often leaving finance and accounting fragmented across multiple business units and technology platforms. According to CFO Research Services, finance organisations that reduce transaction processing focus and reallocate time to enhanced decision-support activity are more likely to be viewed as value-added contributors to strategic and operational decision-making. At the same time, finance must improve the processes and tools within decision support in order to optimise the output. Leading decision support practices include modelling the impact of financial and non-financial measures on shareholder value, deploying these value metrics in key decision-making activities, implementing web-based planning and reporting tools, and enhancing the skills of finance personnel.

Outsourcing is an attractive strategy to accelerate cost and process improvements, while providing access to thought leaders who help CFOs develop proactive strategies that increase shareholder value. According to the CFO Research Services study, finance organisations spend less time on transaction processing by employing leading practices like consolidated and integrated financial systems and shared services. The same study also found that finance could meet the demands placed on it by its various constituencies only by successfully executing the full transformation agenda of cost efficiency and shareholder value improvements. According to research analysts Gartner, CFOs are anxious to experiment on business process outsourcing (BPO) initiatives.

BPO delivers higher-quality business processes at a lower cost by delegating back-office business processes and related technology to an external provider.

A major component of BPO involves finance and accounting outsourcing, the management of the transaction processing and procedure-driven functions of finance and accounting business units. According to a survey by CFO Magazine and AMR Research, the most widely adopted forms of BPO include employee benefits administration, travel services, payroll processing, tax processing, recruitment and collections. The survey found BPO is already popular among companies of all sizes, with 68.3 per cent of respondents engaged in some form of BPO, and 63.6 per cent anticipating an increase over the next year. Gartner forecasts that the worldwide market for process management, the core component of BPO contracts, will grow from $71.3 billion in 2001 to $113.9 billion in 2006.

In successful outsourcing engagements, providers own and manage the processes according to defined metrics, known as service level agreements (SLAs). To establish SLAs the client and the provider must first quantify and measure existing business processes and controls, then define goals for improvements. The provider is then accountable to ensure adherence, often at a significantly improved level over a company's existing compliance. The client company retains responsibility for strategy and policy making, while the provider manages the day-to-day process operations and advises on best practices and process improvement. Both parties are responsible for managing the outsourcing relationship. By outsourcing transactional finance and accounting functions, management can focus on strategic business support activities.

Most companies derive both strategic and tactical benefits from finance and accounting, although specific outcomes are unique to each outsourcing engagement. Traditionally, companies looked to outsourcing primarily to reduce or contain costs. Today, economies of scale are readily achieved from providers with established processing centres and access to offshore talent pools, and more companies use outsourcing as a strategy to improve focus on core business initiatives.

When it comes to finance and accounting, outsourcing typically delivers more consistent, accurate and timely data, with greater control over the processes and improved policy enforcement. Managers and executives can spend their time and energy creating solutions and anticipating markets, rather than compiling a patchwork of financial data generated from multiple sources at periodic intervals.

This is achieved by strategic deployment of human resources and use of leading technology with proven scalability, redundancy and security. These are teamed with methods of reengineering business processes, including: standardisation; consolidation; automation; measurability.

Outsourcing not only imbues an organisation with best practices, but also a greater level of integration among processes and technology systems. A good outsourcer brings process experts to drive higher levels of efficiency. For CFOs who want to stay on the leading edge of all processes and continually shape their organisation to drive shareholder value, outsourcing can be the path to freedom, investing more talent in a strategic vision, delivering value directly to the bottom line, and commanding a more powerful presence at the executive table.

Every outsourcing engagement is a co-created relationship with shared responsibility. The client and outsourcing provider must command a clear, realistic view of the inherent risks and challenges in order to fashion strategies collaboratively that mitigate risk, achieve desired outcomes and support the relationship. Compatibility with an outsourcing partner is essential to a successful outsourcing relationship. Choosing a partner with the capabilities to deliver services to meet business needs requires hefty doses of self-reflection and due diligence. When considering an outsourcing engagement, ask and answer several key questions that need to be asked and answered (see Figure 2.15).

Remember, the best conceived plans change. Unforeseen factors will drive the need for different solutions to those anticipated when the contract was signed. The capacity to anticipate and address change as a team is a critical component of successful outsourcing engagements. Flexibility is a requirement, not only in the contract, but in how both teams communicate, solve problems and achieve strategic goals.

When evaluating outsourcing, ask:

- *Which functions do we want to outsource? Why?*
- *How will outsourcing contribute to corporate mission?*
- *How well does the provider understand our business?*
- *Can the provider's solution be customised to our business?*
- *Can the provider meet our geographic needs?*
- *What is the provider's growth strategy? Can it support our business growth?*
- *How does the provider's culture fit with ours?*
- *Are members of the provider's day-to-day management team effective communicators?*
- *Is the provider's approach flexible and collaborative?*
- *How well does the provider's solution accommodate unforeseen change?*
- *What do existing clients say about the provider?*

Figure 2.15 Key questions when considering outsourcing

2.7

Human Resources

The perfect partner for business process outsourcing

Cost control and effective, efficient working practices strongly influence profit levels in today's business environment. As a result, more organisations are opting to outsource non-core activities. In continuation of a trend that started with IT and communications services, many are outsourcing entire business processes such as human resources and payroll activities. Human resources business process outsourcing (HR BPO) is definitely growing. An analysis of research firm Gartner's statistics suggests HR BPO is achieving a compound annual growth rate of 8.6 per cent, making it the fastest-growing segment of BPO, as more businesses look for benefits beyond outsourcing HR payroll or recruitment.

Although growing, concerns around continuity and reliability are causing some businesses to err on the side of caution. Here, a strategic partner that can work collaboratively with the business can deliver services that are reliable, flexible and designed to scale with the business.

In terms of concerns, salary and personnel administrations are characterised by a stream of innumerable forms, printouts, daily transactions and the need for extensive information exchange with all kinds of bodies and institutions. These are business processes that demand high levels of accuracy, strict discipline and continuity. Research shows that some 60 per cent of all HR tasks are administrative in nature.

It is hardly surprising that large numbers of organisations have decided to outsource their salary administration to specialist companies, but deviations from the letter of contract can lead to high extra costs and many corporations are finding that salary administration goes only part of the way towards alleviating the pressure of mountains of HR administration. The big outsourcing players are now moving into the HR outsourcing market, offering individually tailored company schemes that are neither brand nor package dependent, with total flexibility, transparent pricing and an exhaustive knowledge of regulations, legislation and terms and conditions of employment.

Like many parts of the business where multiple sub-processes of a function coexist, there are numerous options for outsourcing. For HR BPO they can range from using a single multi-process strategic partner, a blend of separate sub-process specialists, or a single collaborative provider that uses an alliance network to leverage local specialists globally. Sub-process specialists can focus on delivering best-practice processes such as functional management (terms and conditions, legislative changes and so on) and transaction processing (such as overtime and bonuses) at a local level.

There are clear advantages in the one-stop-shop approach, such as ease of management and economies of scale but it is essential to choose a partner wisely. Establish the right relationship and the outsourcing partner can manage the entire process (see Figure 2.16), starting with routine tasks such as processing transactions; generating wage and payroll statements; paying out withheld contributions; and producing all kinds of reports. These companies work fast and the client has the opportunity to approve a test run before final processing takes place.

Outsourcing can also cover the administrative HR processes that have to take place prior to salary processing, such as recalculating commuting allowances when employees move house and deciding if salaries qualify for private health insurance or fall under the compulsory state health insurance scheme. Partners should be capable of handling more complex HR tasks too, for example, seizure of salary, or setting up company-sponsored home PC projects, plus offer expert advice on how to best set up a personnel and salary administration.

HR activity fulfilment	Transaction processing	Support	Functional management	Projects/Consultancy
Appointment of new employees	Checking and processing home PC project transactions	General questions relating to HR tasks	Central bargaining agreements' terms and conditions of employment	Transition from traditional collective bargaining agreements to flexible collective bargaining agreements
Collective insurance, such as health insurance, vehicle insurance etc.	Checking and processing submitted overtime sheets	Answering queries concerning payroll statements and transaction processing	Management of underlying data tables	Creating reports
Determining employees' entitlement to health insurance allowances	Checking and processing submitted end of year bonus transactions	Performing calculations at the request of HR, company management, the finance department and employees	Organisational and functional data	Generating handbooks (HR) and making them available on-line
Informing employees about the transition from the compulsory state health insurance scheme to private health insurance and vice versa	Checking and processing deductions for seizure of salary	Handling questions/requests from external bodies	Authorisation management	Interfaces (various options)
Managing sub-administrations (e.g. company saving schemes, seizure of salary, lease cars)	Checking and processing cash advances	Home PC projects (e.g advice on financing)	Modification of existing reports	Education and training (various options)
Managing and administering pension schemes	Checking and processing long service awards	Advice on planned changes in legislation, central bargaining issues, etc.	Implementing legislation changes	Support with (EDP) audits
Administration of cash suspense accounts' blocked accounts	Checking and processing insurance trabsactions	Advice on expatriate allowances and the fiscal aspects thereof	Collective transactions	Writing social plans

Figure 2.16 HR outsourcing services

Some outsourcers offer a highly-qualified service desk that functions as an extension of the client organisation, staffed by employees capable of handling a wide range of questions. Telephone calls or emails to the service desk are answered by first-line or second-line employees, or by a consultant, depending on the difficulty and nature of the query. Consultants can offer advice to your HR employees or line managers, for example on flexible employment contracts.

Tax and social security legislation, and legislation in a wide range of other employment-related areas, is subject to continual change. Good outsourcing partners should have a strong team of specialist consultants, with extensive, up-to-date knowledge of legislation, central bargaining agreements, and terms and conditions of employment. Look for consultants who are not merely there to answer queries, but who proactively analyse and relate any changes relevant to the individual business, such as new central bargaining agreements and can quickly advise on the financial consequences of proposals made during such negotiations.

All things considered, the future for HR BPO looks strong. It is the fastest-growing segment of BPO with rapid growth in offshore capabilities expected. For customers, choosing the right partner is key. Whether the solution is a single, collaborative partner or a network of HR specialists, success is in choosing a provider that offers reliability, regional knowledge and scalability to match the business (see Figure 2.17).

Ideal attributes for an HR outsourcing partner	Key questions for an HR outsourcing partner
Delivery: Regional HR presence, joined-up and backed-up delivery framework with flexible capacity.	What is the global scalability of HR services, eg for coping with merger and acquisition strategies?
Savings: Cost saving strategies that leverage low-cost shared services centres, process optimisation and technology automation.	How much could I expect to save by automating transactional HR processes?
Locations: Multiple locations or partners that can deliver best-practice, low-cost HR services. Local or regional knowledge is key.	What impact could a multi-geography delivery strategy have on my HR function and what sub-processes are suitable for offshore delivery?
Experience: Demonstrable history of providing multi-process HR services in a number of geographic locations.	What scope of processes can you deliver and how mature is your delivery structure?
Collaboration: A history of working with businesses to develop a strategic HR solution jointly.	Is there any flexibility in the way HR services are delivered, and how do they cater for changes in my business?

Figure 2.17 Questions and answers on HR outsourcing

2.8

Supply Chain Management

A case for transformational outsourcing

Chief executives have come to realise that customer satisfaction and business results can be significantly affected by supply chain performance. If a supply chain performing at optimum capacity and efficiency is a foundation for competitive advantage and a lever for shareholder value, the corollary of a poor supply chain is also true. This makes the supply chain a major management task. Supply chains are no longer linear, but are highly complex, collaborative and blurred. Add to this the fact that companies are competing in a volatile economic environment and are finding it increasingly difficult to forecast the future performance of their businesses and markets, and the complexity increases.

The challenge is how to build and manage a complex but adaptive supply chain that maintains agility and delivers consistent ongoing performance, as the business environment continues to evolve. A network-enabled supply chain extends beyond the typical, sequential approach to supply chain management, which is characterised by optimisation of individual functional areas like demand planning, inventory management, and transportation management. Instead, it simultaneously considers all functions within the supply chain as part of the optimisation, incorporating innovative use of business processes, and systems to integrate demand and supply management dynamically.

Moving from a sequential to a network-enabled supply chain is expensive and difficult to execute independently. The conversion needs to be done at the enterprise level and few companies can afford to devote their best resources across the supply chain to enable this kind of business transformation. As some corporations have found, the reality of trying to do this internally is separate, tactical decisions made at various levels throughout the organisation, leading to limited flexibility and unmanaged results.

The technology infrastructure involved in the supply chain is so costly that there is considerable advantage in leveraging the economies of scale and expertise of an outsourcer. Thus, many companies are finding that they can achieve transformation at unprecedented speed through outsourcing. By transferring supply chain processes and staff to a full-service outsourcer, companies tend to gain greater savings with a rapid return on investment and the outsourcer can remove significant risk using service level agreements (see Figure 2.18).

- *Tapping into unrealised cost savings through leveraged sourcing*
- *Adding value by converting operations from overhead to a competitive strength*
- *Decreasing supplier costs by leveraging volume discounts, objectivity and reduced cycle times*
- *Improving inventory performance through sophisticated statistical techniques*
- *Outpacing competition through leading-edge technology and best practices*
- *Avoiding the leakage that surfaces after short-term technology or process improvement initiatives*
- *Freedom to focus on core business such as new product development or winning new customers.*

Figure 2.18 The benefits of transformational outsourcing

Until recently, companies have focused on improving one supply chain process at a time, perhaps procurement, transportation or inventory management. To introduce a network-enabled supply chain, a company needs to focus across the entire supply value chain, incorporating process, technology and resources into a transformation roadmap (see Figure 2.19).

A unique set of skills and capabilities are needed to build and maintain a network-enabled supply chain, with innovative use of technology and integration of systems. Outsourcing allows companies to tap into highly-skilled resources, advanced technology and road-maps that can be customised, enabling supply chain transformation at a surprising speed. Outsourcing to experts that understand the company's industry and can implement integrated solutions is also critical to success.

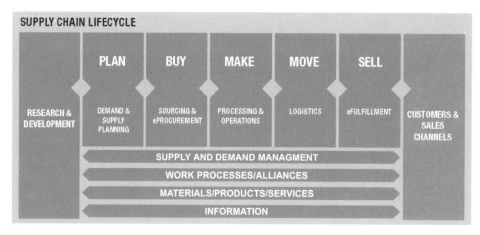

Figure 2.19 Supply chain lifecycle

Effective demand and supply planning is the centrepiece of a network-enabled supply chain. New technologies and management approaches in this area have created exciting opportunities for companies in every industry.

Yesterday, management teams were focused on accurately forecasting demand or accessing demand signals as sales or consumption occurred, with purchasing and production synchronised to demand patterns as accurately as possible.

Today, the approach is shifting to managing demand based on upstream supply chain visibility. Supply chain management and customer relationship management are converging to generate new profit and revenue growth opportunities, but to realise these often requires changes to fundamental business and operating models. New management processes and technologies must be combined with effective integration between customers and trading partners. Outsourcing these functions requires strong collaboration capabilities to ensure that the affected functional areas work seamlessly.

Some outsourcing partners extend their services to the transformation of purchasing power, achieving reduced costs for externally sourced goods and services. Transforming sourcing and e-procurement functions can reduce an organisation's direct cost of goods and services, while decreasing cycle time and improving supplier relationships and product quality (see Figure 2.20).

Tap into world-class talent and leading technology to transform the supply chain into a strategic advantage. Key questions to consider:

- *Are you concerned about the rising costs of operating your supply chain?*
- *Are your people world-class supply chain experts?*
- *Are you getting the full benefits and using the complete functionality of your supply chain software?*
- *Can you keep up to date with new releases of software?*
- *How can your organisation achieve more consistent supply chain performance?*
- *How can you get a more guaranteed expenditure for your supply chain?*

Figure 2.20 Transforming the supply chain

Essentially, this is achieved using internet technologies to develop and deploy strategies that connect suppliers and improve the bottom line. By consolidating buying volumes, negotiating improved pricing, managing suppliers and improving catalogue maintenance, business processes are significantly streamlined, company profits enhanced and customer expectations exceeded.

Meeting customer expectations is a major achievement, but it must be coupled to improved profit. As the balance of power shifts from manufacturers and suppliers to more demanding customers, world-class companies realise that customers want to buy superior products that are perfectly delivered. To achieve these goals, companies must focus on the integration of products, information, delivery methods and cash flow.

Leading-edge outsourcers offer the perfect answer: a comprehensive logistics and e-fulfilment solution that encompasses supply chain processes from the time the customer places the order to the time when the product is delivered and paid for. While the order-to-payment process seems simple to the customer, for the company the solution can be fraught with challenges. A few corporations have achieved it with an outsourced, end-to-end fulfilment solution that provides total supply chain visibility, connectivity to trading partners and the ability to manage and optimise physical delivery. Such solutions focus on the customer and synchronise partners and drivers across the entire supply chain (see Figure 2.21).

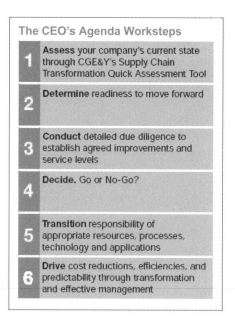

Figure 2.21 The CEO's agenda for outsourcing supply chain management

These possibilities show that, for most companies, the supply chain is one of the most untapped and significant opportunities for gaining sustained competitive advantage (as in the case study described in Figure 2.22). But using innovative technologies, streamlined processes and improved collaboration with supply chain partners, companies can dramatically reduce costs, improve inventory turns and cycle times and, ultimately, generate new sources of free cash flow. By outsourcing these functions, they can achieve these benefits more quickly with less risk, lower cost and a much higher probability of success.

Business Issue

Full market liberalisation of the Canadian energy sector was fast approaching and an owner and operator of one of the 10 largest transmission and distribution systems in North America needed to streamline its business in order to be competitive in the new market conditions. One specific business area requiring transformation to reduce costs while increasing efficiency was the supply chain.

Capgemini was selected as the company's outsourcing provider, supplying a range of IT and business processes including supply chain, customer care, finance and certain transactional human resources services. Through the agreement, Capgemini acts as an agent with purchasing authority, assumes day-to-day responsibility for third-party managed contracts, manages inbound and outbound transportation processes, and is responsible for inventory planning and management.

To drive supply chain efficiencies, Capgemini restructured the company's supply management function into focused teams: strategic sourcing, purchasing and demand management and logistics. In addition, Capgemini launched four transformational enhancement projects:

- *Supply chain – logistics optimisation*

- *Procurement – requisition to payment, processes*

- *Leverage IT infrastructure*

- *Reverse logistics – investment recovery*

Figure 2.22 Case study: supply chain outsourcing

2.9

Business Fusion

In search of business optimisation and flexibility

Business fusion is driving a revolution in efficiency as it melds business processes and IT. Essentially, it involves delivering end-to-end business processes, such as purchase-to-pay, from integrated IT and business process management infrastructures. Research analysts Gartner describe it as enabling new compound processes that provide coherent control of activities that have previously been loosely linked. The result is greater business optimisation and flexibility.

Implementing integrated IT solutions, such as enterprise resource planning (ERP) systems, for various back-office and business functions is not new. But business fusion moves forward to combine existing systems and integrate data and business sub-processes for real-time functionality, and this is much more difficult. It requires a single, integrated business and IT strategy, management of sub-process chains as one process and the ability to trace data from one end of an integrated process chain to the other. For many companies, creating and managing such an environment is expensive, time-consuming and complex.

Outsourcing is one option for developing business fusion as it can deploy and optimise integrated business processes quickly. Service providers invest heavily to deliver multiple processes across common IT architectures from low-cost shared service centres, making them prime candidates for the task. From the business point of view, a single strategic partner for both business process and IT management is key in achieving performance evolution and reduced costs, by simplifying service procurement and delivery.

If the early wins from business fusion are efficiency, flexibility, and reduced costs, the strategic gain is in the improved management of business outcomes. This is pivotal to trading in volatile environments: first, autonomous business sub-processes that are closely linked for service-oriented control are more flexible under significant change, such as market or industry transformation; second, fusion promotes enterprise-wide cost to serve reduction, rather than total cost of ownership, by being able to reconcile end-to-end delivery costs against functional and process enhancements; and finally fusion allows the enterprise to become more efficient by consolidating the functionality of business systems to gain process and data management efficiencies that cannot be achieved through disparate data flows.

Fusion is being made possible by advancements in application pervasiveness and connectivity, and is resolving two key issues that prevented business fusion from happening previously.

First, many enterprises captured insufficient transactional data to enable any meaningful links or integration. This shortfall is solved by more mature and pervasive enterprise-class applications that connect and capture transactional data, such as SAP, Siebel or Peoplesoft. These operate fewer data dictionaries with greater data efficiencies and are aimed at integrating specific IT and business processes.

The second barrier to fusion was the incompatibility of applications. But applications and architectures that link high-level management processes and provide speed and information flow for management decision support software are becoming available in the form of See-Beyond, MS BizTalk and Oracle ProcessConnect. These technologies underpin the flexibility that fusion provides by reducing the complexity and cycle times of business processes, connecting disparate data sources from trading partners, web e-commerce applications and legacy systems, and enabling easier access to real-time management data.

With the obstacles in fusion overcome, the requirements of business and IT transformation come into view, raising outsourcing as an option to tackle the challenge. Outsourcing provides access to previous investment in applications, shared service centres, skills and transformation experience. But, it does require a fundamentally different approach as IT and business strategies become one. This means the scope of outsourcing should incorporate the end-to-end business process and supporting IT.

For outsourced business fusion to work, service vendors must be aligned, and the most effective way to achieve this is through a single multi-skilled partner. Such a partner provides efficiencies that cannot be gained through a multi-vendor arrangement, by managing services centrally, having common business and IT goals, and writing risk and reward contracts based on business outcome.

Although expensive and difficult to achieve, transformational outsourcing can provide flexible commercial models that spread the cost of such change over many years (see Figure 2.23).

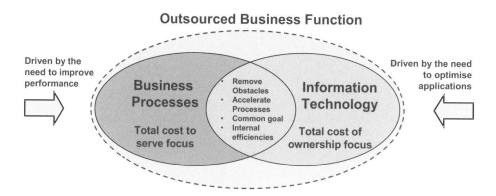

Figure 2.23 The gains of business fusion

Key success factors for outsourcing business fusion include the use of sole source outsourcing for IT and business processes, end-to-end process modelling and automation through enabling technology. A greater emphasis on outsourcing partnerships is also advantageous, underpinning the trend towards risk and reward commercial arrangements.

Fusion requires considerable skills in applications integration and architecture restructuring, and relies on a clear and robust business process management framework to guide transformation towards integration.

Ongoing delivery of business fusion services requires a similar joint effort between the business and IT, while sole source outsourcing arrangements will provide communication and co-ordination between process and IT management.

With the route to business fusion unrolling and outsourcers ready to take up the task, the benefits are there to be taken.

Part Three

Successful Outsourcing

Introduction

Outsourcing arrangements, like mergers and acquisitions, are often large and complex, strategically and operationally important, and involve significant organisational strain – but effective use of outsourcing can be a critical component in corporate success for many companies.

Different activities are outsourced in different ways to achieve different objectives. Experience shows that, irrespective of what is outsourced, why and how, the key to success is collaboration. This must be fuelled by quality relationships between all parties; relationships based on clearly defined, top-down, aligned goals; and flexibility to meet changing needs.

Collaboration is no longer just amicably working together. Now it is about truly combining skills and strengths to accelerate the benefits of outsourcing for an organisation's business.

Succeeding is not easy and there are examples of public and private sector deals not delivering to expectations. Those that do succeed share three common attributes: clarity of expectations; an enduring and mutually advantageous relationship; and agility to embrace change.

Outsourcing can achieve a wide spectrum of objectives, ranging from doing the same things at a lower cost – traditional outsourcing – to achieving new things in new ways – transformational outsourcing. If the vision is up-front, with clear and achievable expectations, an outsourcing strategy can articulate the vision.

One component of this strategy must be to fit the deal structure and the relationship to the objectives. The commercials, including the reward structure, must reflect the business goals, apportionment of risk and the desires of the relationship. Having a clear approach to governing the relationship – mutually defined and widely accepted – will act as an accelerator for success.

There must also be built-in flexibility and one eye on change. Change is inevitable in most cases of outsourcing – in fact, outsourcing is itself a form of change for an organisation and the arrangement needs to have an appropriate level of built-in flexibility to ensure the service and relationship continually function efficiently. This is especially critical for transformational outsourcing, where the business change team, the new technology team and the service delivery team must be aligned in their objectives and approach.

3.1

Defining an Outsourcing Strategy

Selecting components for a successful strategy

The options of outsourcing are broadening, the complexity expanding and the consequences, both positive and negative, are growing in magnitude. Making the right decision on outsourcing is critical and developing an effective outsourcing strategy that is integral to the business strategy is the key to success.

Nowadays, outsourcing is multi-dimensional, with techniques such as business process and transformational services providing benefits on many fronts. This diversity leads organisations to encounter many questions when considering a suitable approach for outsourcing (see Figure 3.1). But there is no single, correct answer to questions about what should be outsourced, and which is the best provider.

However, the answers do depend on two fundamental aspects: what is the aim of outsourcing, and is this within the context of the organisation and its goals. By initially considering these two questions, organisations are able to set the direction for developing an outsourcing strategy.

Figure 3.1 Approaches to outsourcing

The decision-making process needs to ensure that inputs to the strategy are all-inclusive and relevant. Many contributions will be needed from across the business, ranging from market views and corporate goals through to the desires of various stakeholders such as senior executives and business managers. With this accountability for the process in mind, an 'outsourcing champion' becomes a possibility. Depending on the scale and shape of the strategy, this role could be latched onto another, or perhaps a new role of chief outsourcing officer created.

The contents of the strategy will always be specific to every organisation, but the fundamental reasoning will always be the same, outsourcing must be beneficial in line with business goals. To determine whether this is the case, the why, what, where and who of outsourcing must be considered. By candidly answering these questions, organisations can outline the principles of their strategy.

'What are you trying to achieve with outsourcing?' is the alternative question to 'why consider outsourcing?' While the initial answers will differ depending on whom you are asking, it is objectives aligned with the corporate goals that must be identified for the outsourcing strategy.

For example, the chief executive officer may be considering organisational change, while the chief operating officer's priority will be operational efficiency. Similarly, the chief financial officer may be looking for lower costs and better value, while the chief information officer is seeking to access new or specialist skills to implement new technologies. All these drivers are significant and must be pooled together and then distilled when defining the strategy (see Figure 3.2)

In terms of what to outsource, this will depend on the business. Every organisation has a business value chain that is used to create a product or service for an end-customer; and every element within this chain could be a candidate for outsourcing, but outsourcing everything is not the answer. Indeed, reaching the right answer is further complicated as the traditional outsourcing argument of core versus non-core is no longer the only option.

- **Financial** – cost reduction, cost avoidance, financial restructuring – fixed versus variable clarity in expenditure

- **Quality** – improvements in service, stricter governance, application of best practices and tools, tackling resource shortfalls and new skills

- **Business** – focus on core business, flexibility to embrace change, clear service accountability

- **People** – control of staffing costs, management of staff churn, leveraging experience, access to specialists

- **Technology** – capitalise on vendor and industry initiatives, realisation of technological benefits.

Figure 3.2 Reasons to outsource

The common types of outsourcing – conventional, problem-solving and transformational (see Figure 3.3) – offer the capability to address different business objectives ranging from traditional cost reduction through to major change. By mapping the organisation's goals and desires with these capabilities, an approach to using outsourcing will become meaningful.

The scope of modern outsourcing covers a much wider spectrum offering the opportunity to sharpen business operations by using some or all of the services of business process outsourcing, such as finance and accounting, human resources, customer relationship management, and IT outsourcing.

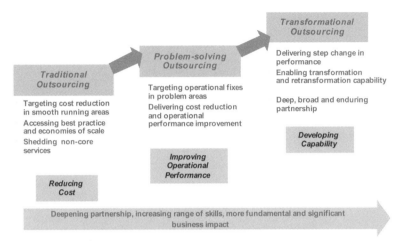

Figure 3.3 Types of outsourcing

Identifying which elements to outsource and which to retain in-house can be difficult. This difficulty can be resolved however, by considering the importance of the element to the business, the ability of the element to meet the organisations' business goals and the corporate stance on outsourcing.

For example, if shedding non-core elements is imperative, elements that are of low importance to the business should be outsourced. In this case, a conventional outsourcing model could be suitable to remove the distraction of low importance activities from the business.

Similarly, if the ability to change within budget constraints is an imperative, prime candidates for outsourcing would be value chain elements that are of high importance to the business, but are too costly and risky to change using existing methods. A transformational outsourcing model would be the most suitable option here.

Further, organisations should challenge the entire business structure and, for each element, justify the business reasons for outsourcing – or not. The scope of what to outsource is driven by the organisation's attitude to outsourcing and its appetite to change elements of the business that cause difficulty in meeting its business goals.

Having decided what to outsource, it is important to consider where the processing should be done. Traditionally, within mature economic regions, outsourcing provided remote delivery of services from supplier locations within the regions, for example, a UK client company would use a UK-resourced supplier.

The move to low-cost labour centres introduced areas, such as India, has created further solutions for remote delivery around the offshore concept (see Figure 3.4). Other countries have seized this opportunity with Southern and Eastern Europe, Latin America and the Far East becoming viable options. As the outsourcing industry evolves, with separation of service provision from service location becoming the norm, oganisations face additional choices on how to use locations of service to their advantage.

Figure 3.4 Locations to benefit the business

Choosing a location onsite, in-country, nearshore, farshore or even a blend of these approaches is a possibility and documenting the right approach to locations becomes a requirement of the outsourcing strategy (see Figure 3.5).

The strategy must also include core criteria for choosing the right partners, based on their ability to deliver the service. However, equally significant to capability and experience are partners with whom the client organisation is comfortable in its dealings. Therefore, defining the value-added or soft-skill attributes of potential partners becomes a necessity for the outsourcing strategy. Some of these attributes, such as business ethics, can be difficult to measure clinically, but having a clear view of expectations will lay the foundations for a successful working relationship.

- **Regulatory requirements** – *can data cross boundaries, if so is this restricted to certain regions such as the European Union? Do the locations comply with audit, industry and insurance regulations?*

- **Quality of the local labour market** – *education, qualification and experience level of personnel*

- **Flexibility to scale** – *can remote centres scale in line with expected growth and how would the centres cope with unusual peaks in work load?*

- **Language requirements** – *if there is a requirement for multiple European languages then low-cost European regions such as Spain and Poland may be preferential to the Indian sub-continent*

- **Right risk profile** – *consider the political and environmental stability of the location, as well as how business continuity and disaster recovery will be handled*

- **Default position** – *should offshore be first choice, followed by other options or is a blend of offshore and onshore the best option?*

Figure 3.5 Making the location decision

Every organisation will have a different view as to what constitutes an ideal partner and these views, along with their importance, should be included in the outsourcing strategy. Common attributes to consider include: delivery capability; business empathy; track record; innovation; culture; industry leadership; and risk.

A supplementary consideration is whether to use multiple suppliers or a single supplier. Multiple suppliers can create an element of competition that inevitably stimulates commercial and solution creativity. However, they require a higher degree of management than a single supplier. Additionally, a single supplier can be integrated deeply with an organisation, creating a high degree of collaboration. The warning here is that this can lead to dependency and uncompetitiveness.

A combination of multiple and single suppliers can be used depending on the circumstances. For example, smaller discrete elements can be outsourced to multiple specialists, while larger change-driven programmes can be outsourced to a single supplier.

While the individual decisions in defining an outsourcing strategy are important, it is essential that deriving the strategy goes hand-in-hand with the overall corporate development process. The outsourcing strategy should not be developed as a stand-alone initiative and must be driven top-down with the underlying purpose of supporting what is best for the business (see Figure 3.6).

The strategy must also include core criteria for choosing the right partners, based on their ability to deliver the service. However, equally significant to capability and experience are partners with whom the client organisations is comfortable in its dealings. Therefore, defining the value-added or soft-skill attributes of potential partners becomes a necessity for the outsourcing strategy. Some of these attributes, such as business ethics, can be difficult to measure clinically, but having a clear view of expectations will lay the foundations for a successful working relationship.

It is here that the chief outsourcing officer comes into play, considering the outsourcing strategy for the whole enterprise. The chief outsourcing officer should work alongside existing business functions and have the flexibility to create solutions using whatever outsourcing solutions best meet the business need. The outsourcing officer can also be complemented by an intermediary outsourcing specialist who can provide independent expert guidance.

The outsourcing strategy must:

- *Be integral to the corporate strategy, including the strategy development process*

- *Target clearly defined business objectives with specific types of outsourcing*

- *Set out a corporate outsourcing approach covering global requirements, locations of service, commercial structures and an overall timeline of execution*

- *Define at a high level what should and should not be outsourced with objective reasoning*

- *Highlight organisational requirements to facilitate outsourcing, including the procurement process, and implementation resources such as an outsourcing team or chief outsourcing officer*

- *Focus on cultural fit as well as strategic fit.*

Figure 3.6 Critical successful factors

From Thought to Outsource

Turning the theories of outsourcing into reality

The process

Once the decision to outsource has been made, there are four distinct steps to move to a managed service delivered by a third-party specialist (see Figure 3.7). Traditionally, the process involves significant bottom-up activity, but we are increasingly seeing a top-down approach similar in nature to mergers and acquisitions. The challenge is to blend speed and rigour.

Scoping

The first step along the path to outsourcing is scoping the business objectives.

This defines the objectives for the deal, develops a high-level, but robust, understanding of the scope and key constraints, and understands the human resources implications of outsourcing.

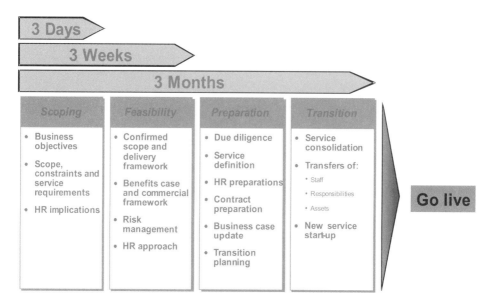

Figure 3.7 The four stages of the outsourcing process

The business objectives define a common understanding of the goals for the potential outsourcing relationship and a high-level definition of the economics and commercial implications. The business objectives provide the context for everything that follows, making this stage key to setting the tone of a partnership with a service provider and making sure the provider can work collaboratively towards aligned goals.

Once the business objectives are defined, it is necessary to identify what is in and out of scope, and to set an initial overview of key constraints and service requirements. Again, this is a critical early phase, that sets boundaries for much of the work that follows. Definitions of service requirements are about understanding the answers to the what, where, when and how questions of ongoing delivery and these will have implications.

By the end of this phase, there will be a clear understanding of the shape of the solution and the extent to which it can meet business objectives. But it will trigger human resources implications, for example, moving activities offshore often means redundancies. The goal of this phase is to understand these implications so that they can be factored into the business case and future planning.

Feasibility

Feasibility moves to the next level of detail. It develops a more detailed and robust understanding of the scope, a second level business case, and begins to outline the commercial principles of the deal. This stage is neither linear nor parallel. All of the phases integrate and there needs to be a process to make them work together. At the end of this stage, the business case and scope are clearer and the team is ready to shift the emphasis into planning activities.

Feasibility builds on the initial scope and constraints to define the next level of detail. It sets out the delivery framework and the implications for the business case, supporting risk management activities by providing robust boundaries for the transition.

The feasibility phase also covers the benefits case, setting the context for the proposed delivery and the commercial agenda by drawing out key parameters of the service delivery on which the pricing strategy can be based.

The scoping stage highlighted constraints to the scope and business case. Risk management develops this into a risk register and defines who is responsible for risk and how it will be mitigated. The key is to revisit this issue throughout the process to ensure risks are effectively contained or mitigated as they move up the critical list. A common understanding of risk also ensures that both client and provider work together to contain it – a shared vision provides the best possible view of risk containment.

Human resources must also be considered as part of feasibility, with a review looking at potential approaches and reaching a way forward aligned with the business objectives and delivery framework. A communication plan that supports the preparation and transition phases is important here.

Preparation

The preparation phase is about moving to definitions of service that can be laid out in a contract and due diligence to confirm assumptions and assets. There are significant degrees of freedom in the approach to this stage, but they carry substantial impact in terms of speed and risk, making it essential to find the right balance.

Preparation must first confirm assumptions from the scoping and feasibility stages through due diligence. This validates critical facts and details, and can result in alterations to the delivery and commercial frameworks, and to the business case. Validated information underpins both the contractual agreement and the transition plan, such as the number of staff or assets in scope and the measured service delivery on which contractual percentage improvements are based.

Service definition then identifies the objectives, roles, responsibilities and processes associated with the end solution. It defines a level of detail that can be contracted and sets the parameters for the transition plan – an unambiguous statement of deliverables that supports the contract and commercial framework, and is the basis for creating the transition plan.

The nature of due diligence in the preparation stage means that changes may be required and some may be significant. Due diligence can go as far as triggering changes to the business case, benefits case and commercial framework. This is a critical milestone in keeping the transfer aligned to business objectives.

The contract is the legal document that sets out working boundaries for the partnership between the client and the service provider. It builds on the parameters of the service definition and service requirements, and aligns joint expectations for the future. It is paramount to have a contract that fits the type of outsourcing arrangement that is being prepared.

For example, transformational outsourcing requires a contract that supports flexibility and change, whereas traditional outsourcing will suit a more rigid contract based on service level agreements.

However, change is guaranteed and contracts are never future proof. Sharing the vision and strategy of the business during the negotiations can help ensure that the outsourced service can be adapted in the near future. Top-level goals and rewards and penalties that capture both parties' definitions of commercial success need to be spelt out, with the balance of certainty and flexibility remaining the Holy Grail.

Both parties must also take responsibility for transition planning. This creates an actionable list of goals and tasks for executing the business transfer, setting joint responsibility for the transfer and driving all actions throughout the transition phase. It builds on outputs from the due diligence phase to plan for differences in geography and the how and when of physically moving assets, and is best achieved in terms of responsibilities and accountability with a combined and dedicated transition team.

Moving on to human resources preparations, it is necessary to define an actionable level of detail for the HR communication plan, as well as initiate communication of the business transfer to staff, unions and workers' councils. This is best achieved following transition planning and contract preparation, to ensure communications are accurate and it is the first real step to effecting transition. By executing communication collaboratively and keeping staff involved, staff morale and productivity are sustained.

Transition

Transition is the first of the 'just do it' stages. In this phase, transfer of staff, assets and responsibilities to the outsourcing partner takes place – the analysis becomes commercial reality. It is a stressful stage, placing additional strain on already stretched resources and service provision. The key is effective planning, communication and collaborative execution coupled with a reliance on a continued understanding of clear business expectations. Communication is critical, as business expectations are paramount to success.

Any problems that are outsourced are unlikely to be fixed on day one, but a joined-up communication stream ensures both parties have the same expectations.

The first phase of transition prepares the disparate assets, knowledge and processes in scope for transfer as they are, or for consolidation during transfer. It builds on the transition plan by ring-fencing the physical and separating the intangible.

Consolidation of services may require the merging of disparate functions across widely-spread geographic locations. Normally the goal is to enable services to be consolidated in a single transfer. Where geographic constraints apply, such as country-specific regulations that affect how quickly business transfers can happen, consolidation may need to be completed in phases.

Transfer is the moment of truth. It is when staff, assets and responsibilities are actually transferred from the organisation to the outsourcer. It is a difficult and complex time when success is determined by the robustness of transition and communication planning, and the rigour of service consolidation. Staff are closely managed to ensure they are kept motivated and have the information they need, and physical assets are migrated during scheduled and convenient downtimes to prevent service interruption.

At this stage, the contract is finalised and signed, and service responsibility shifts to the outsourcer. How smoothly this happens depends on transfer of knowledge and keeping staff motivated and involved.

With everything and everybody in place, service start-up tests and measures transferred services against business expectations, providing joint assurance that the transfer was a success and setting the tone for ongoing service management. Where problems have been outsourced, they are unlikely to be resolved immediately, as the initial goal is to establish a stabilised environment.

Speed versus certainty

While there is a generic route from thought to outsource, there are degrees of freedom in terms of approach and rigour. The trade-off is between speed and risk, and the time it takes to reach the operating model and its benefits in terms of service level and cost. There is no right answer; the balance needs to be fit for purpose.

Traditionally, companies have taken a bottom-up rigorous approach to outsourcing decisions and this is not surprising. It is a significant step to outsource key activities to a third party and it is essential to know that their activities will be executed appropriately. This requires a substantial degree of detail, but it is important not to confuse detail with certainty.

The bottom-up approach relies on a high degree of due diligence and contractual detail. It relies on the letter of the contract and the detailed specification of assets, typically allowing a few degrees of freedom. The timescale to outsource in this case is usually three to six months.

Because of the level of detailed analysis, this approach is labour intensive, takes longer to complete and is costly, implementation takes longer and the realisation of cost savings is delayed. The balance here is of costs against perceived reduction in risk.

The bottom-up approach is appropriate in highly complex circumstances, or where multiple geographically dispersed services are in scope.

As they race to remove cost increases, companies are seeking accelerated routes to outsourcing. This requires a top-down approach focusing on commercial principles. Typically, both parties will agree a price or cost per unit that is based on a benchmark.

The top-down approach involves much lower due diligence as it is based on the principle of delivering a service to an agreed volume, often with an agreement to scale the volume and cost to meet business objectives. In this way the complete thought to outsource process can be compressed into three months.

This approach is much less labour intensive and faster to arrange as less detail is necessary. There is still a strong collaborative need to plan for and execute the transfer, but the emphasis is on the critical path. It is beneficial where high business growth is expected.

Accelerating the process involves collaborative tools and methods. One catalyst will be an environment designed to share knowledge and fuel decision-making, such as an accelerated solutions environment. This is an artificial environment, normally offsite, where result-focused workshops can be held over a number of days. Stakeholders are brought together in a neutral environment to make collaborative business decisions.

Key to success is bringing together experts to make critical decisions and supporting them with validated information. Qualified decisions can then be reached in a matter of days. As the top-down approach becomes more prevalent, the challenge remains to achieve a balance between time and certainty, cost and results. There is no magic answer – but an outsource has to be done with you, not to you, if it is to be successful.

3.3

Creating a Robust Contract

A quick lesson learnt from experience

Outsourcing is a business relationship with the contract documenting the legal bias of the relationship. Getting the right contract in place is essential for outsourcing and the contract needs to lead the relationship rather than shackle it in legalities. But getting it right is not just about covering all the angles and possibilities; it is about having a contract that is suitable for both the arrangement and the business circumstances.

The contract needs to be compatible with the type of outsourcing being undertaken and reflective of the desired working relationship. For example, a rigid, penalty-based contract may be suitable for a simple service driven by a service level agreement, but this approach would not be suitable for a more complex, change-driven transformational service. In this circumstance, flexibility would need to be introduced into the contract. Flexibility does not necessarily equate with ambiguity. On the contrary, for a contract it stipulates an agreement that allows both sides the ability to propose contract variations to cater for change.

Defining and agreeing the contract

The process for defining and agreeing the contract is equally as important as its content. During this time both the client and supplier begin to form their working relationship, with the outcome of contract negotiations often setting the ongoing tone. By starting as early as possible, basic principles and minor points can be quickly agreed, leaving sufficient time for clarifying the nitty-gritty of the service and agreeing major points.

During the process, third-party outsourcing intermediaries may offer a degree of comfort for client organisations, but care should be taken to ensure that the process of reaching agreement does not become constrained by introducing more layers of involvement. The contents of the contract set out the obligations of the parties and document standard working principles and details of the service. While there is no definition of a 'good' contract, useful attributes include clarity, simplicity of structure, a clear statement of obligations on both sides, an element of mutual agreement, flexibility and freshness in terms of ongoing relevance.

The modular contract

Although the contract will define the rules of the game, both sides should avoid continually getting out the rulebook. Instead, a properly constructed contract will become the framework for the outsourcing relationship and act as the starting point for shaping governance requirements.

In the first instance, the structure of a contract can be used to aid the process of quickly agreeing and documenting the outsourcing service. A suitable approach is to use a modular framework that allows both client and supplier to easily separate constituent parts of a contract into relevant groupings and co-related sections (see Figure 3.8).

The modular structure uses master agreements to cover the core aspects of a contract, with additional sub-agreements for each specific service. It is advisable to use additional sub-agreements for staff transfers owing to their complexity. Supplementary details for each agreement's grouping can then be described within supporting schedules. Handling the people side within separate sub-agreements ensures that the intricate and often emotional nature of staff transfers receives the same prominence as the actual services.

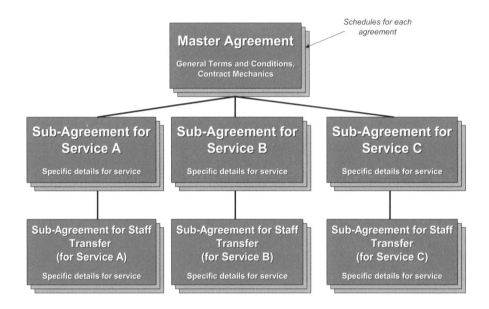

Figure 3.8 A modular contact framework

This approach distinguishes the various service components from each other as well as from the general overall requirements. It then becomes possible to accelerate the developments of the contract by progressing these sections as separate parallel streams. During parallel development the integrity of the contract as a whole is imposed by the interrelationship of the sections within the modular structure. It is essential that each side use a single point of accountability to enforce this integrity, especially if different resources are used to create parts of the contract.

The contract is simpler to navigate and easier to maintain, as each change to a sub-agreement does not necessarily mean a change to other areas. Flexibility is also gained by the ability to add or remove sub-agreements as the service changes (see Figure 3.9).

Master Agreement	• General terms & conditions covering: ○ Term and termination ○ Sub-contracting ○ Intellectual property rights ○ Contract change control and management ○ Escalation process ○ Charging and payment terms ○ Relationship management ○ Liability and indemnity ○ Euro ○ Benchmarking ○ Step-in rights ○ Confidentiality ○ Employee restrictions
Sub-Agreements – Services	• Service specifics including: ○ Hardware and software – which is client supplied, client assigned (ie rented by client and assigned to supplier), transferring to supplier ○ Licensing ○ Service scope – core aspects and additional aspects ○ Service levels ○ Charges ○ Service credits & bonuses ○ Locations of work ○ Security
Sub-Agreements – Staff Transfer	• Human resource specifics including: ○ Client and supplier obligations ○ Pension rights ○ Seconded staff ○ Staff in scope ○ Employment terms & conditions

Figure 3.9 Typical contents of a modular contract

Finalising the contract

The act of signing a contract is the moment of commitment and always seen as a major milestone. Consequently, the finalisation of any outsourcing contract is usually on the critical path of a procurement schedule, and, furthermore, once the contract has been signed its contents have to be rapidly conveyed to staff involved in delivering and using the service, including those managing the relationship.

Most organisations have a defined process to follow when developing a contract, usually in line with a standard procurement practice. Unfortunately, a smooth and trouble-free process is rarely achieved owing to the complexities of reaching agreement. But experience shows there are some pointers that can help the process to reach a rapid and successful conclusion. First, it is wise to start as soon as possible by using a modular contract and use contract negotiations efficiently. The correct people need to be involved and, after signing, the contract needs to be kept in line with changes.

Contracts are often issued during the tendering process to lay out initial positioning and establish broad principles of agreement. This allows early identification of common ground and areas for negotiation, making best use of subsequent dialogue and contract negotiation meetings. By using a modular framework, sections of the contract can be concluded as agreement is reached in the tendering process, avoiding the need to compress contract development between selecting the winning proposal and commencing the service.

Negotiation

Negotiation goes hand-in-hand with contract development to agree the common ground of all parties. However, negotiating can become an inhibitor to the process depending on the stance taken by both sides. The farther apart both sides start, the longer it will take to reach agreement. This makes the process of agreement more costly, especially when employing specialist advisors and legal experts. By accepting from the outset that a contract needs to be mutually agreeable, both sides can save time and expense by beginning negotiations from a position that is nearer to each other and thus nearer to the point of agreement.

Using the right people during the development of the contract is vital. Contract development is not purely the domain of the legal profession, as an outsourcing contract will contain a high level of detail regarding the services to be provided. A multi-disciplined team should drive the development of the contract, with the leader being a contract specialist – a risk and contract manager – who has broad knowledge of legal, commercial and service delivery (see Figure 3.10). Using this type of person allows specialists, who can be expensive resources, to focus on the technicalities of their areas such as legal, service or financial.

Figure 3.10 The role of the risk and contract manager

Using the right people needs to be complemented by clear mapping between client and supplier contract development teams. This ensures that during the later and often frenetic stages of negotiation there is a common understanding of the correct communication channels.

Post-contract performance

Once the contract is signed, it will form the centrepiece of the out-sourcing services as it defines scope and expectations. Therefore its content should be comprehensively cascaded through both client and supplier organisations. This can be done through mutually-agreed mechanisms, such as the governance model, and documentation, such as a statement of work and service level agreements.

During the delivery of the services, it is crucial that both sides accept responsibility for ensuring that the contract continues to remain relevant. Should the contract become misaligned with the service being delivered, both the client and supplier will enter into a range of commercial and legal uncertainties regarding obligations and liability. Contract reviews must be a regular feature, especially when a client is experiencing major change, and should be viewed as constructive to developing the relationship and service (see Figure 3.11).

Do not overload the contract	Resist the temptation to over-engineer the contract, it will only create confusion when trying to understand its contents.
Do not work outside the contract	Asking suppliers to undertake work not covered by the contract is not getting something for nothing. It could develop into legal and commercial uncertainty over what was delivered and who is liable for any failure or unsatisfactory supply. If a contract cannot be agreed in the timescales, consider using a legally binding 'Instruction To Proceed' as short-term cover.
Avoid ambiguous statements	Ambiguous statements like 'agree to agree' introduce unwarranted vagueness into contracts, leading to uncertainty in requirements and obligations.
Be reasonable on liability limitations	Very few suppliers will sign up for unlimited liability. Liabilities need to balance the risk apportionment, be appropriate for the services being supplied and also be reciprocal.
Use service credits appropriately	Applying very large service credits may adversely affect the supplier and its ability to deliver the service. They can have the effect of shifting the focus to service credit management rather than to developing the service. Use such devices as a sharp stick rather than as a sledgehammer.
Be clear on licence ownership	Understand and document in the contract who owns licenses, who is allowed to use them and who is responsible for their maintenance. Incorrectly assuming ownership could lead to suppliers unintentionally breaching vendor copyrights.
Silence is not golden	If something is not explicitly stated in the contract then it is ambiguous. This leads to conflicting assumptions being made by both sides.
Cover the exit	Ensure that the exit or close down of a contract is covered. This includes how it will occur and who pays for what costs depending on the reason for the exit. As this may be many years in the future, all the potential circumstances for exiting may not be known, but at the contract stage the principles can be agreed.
Include reasonable rate increases	Be cognisant that suppliers need to make a return on the service, enabling them to make investments and improvements. Use industry-wide measures to include acceptable increases.
Use contract term and break points as incentives	For example for a seven-year deal, consider offering the supplier five years to invest and improve the service. Then for the final two years reserve the right to explore new suppliers. However, use an incentive option of an extension for a further five years should the supplier prove that it is still the right partner during these final two years.
Ensure obligations are cascaded to sub-contractors and all relevant third parties	Ensure that, in the case of sub-contractors, contractual obligations are correctly passed down using back-to-back agreements.
Use people who will deliver and use the service during the contracting stages	This will start the process of cascading the contents of the contract, providing early buy-in from those using and delivering the service.
Once the contract is in force, manage problems early	Issues should be resolved at service delivery level and only be escalated if all else fails. Both sides should not hide problems and must work together to find a resolution. In the event of a major dispute, mediation is preferred to litigation and is often cheaper.

Figure 3.11 Lessons to learn

3.4

A Structure for Success

Balancing commercial elements of the contract

In an outsourcing arrangement, as in any commercial partnership, building the right commercial structure is critical. The structure drives behaviour and incentivises outcomes. It is, perhaps, the key element of governance and the payment structure must accurately reflect the strategic goals of the deal. If the structure is not appropriate for the arrangement, then the deal will not be set up for success.

Of course, getting the structure right is not straightforward; there are a wide range of possibilities around the strategy for payment and the mechanisms to implement this strategy. In addition, in a long-term deal, there are further choices for financial profiling, such as smoothing out up-front investment costs.

Whilst this choice may mean there are many ways to get it wrong, choice does bring flexibility and many opportunities to get the structure right. A successful commercial solution uses payment mechanisms to achieve the right balance between four core attributes: cost to clients; risk apportionment; business goals; and profitability for the supplier.

Reducing costs is almost always a driver for outsourcing and the commercial structure must accommodate this with an appropriate degree of certainty. Additionally, the payment structure needs to reflect the level of risk being accepted by all parties. This is particularly significant for creative payment structures, such as transaction-based payments, where higher rewards can be used to offset the risk of unpredictable revenue for the supplier. Further, the right commercial solution must align with the goals of the business, not just definitive cost reduction objectives, but also broader goals, such as business change. In all cases, the commercial solution must allow the supplier to turn a profit, not necessarily excessive gains, but enough for the deal to be of interest.

Apart from the simplest outsourcing deals, most need flexibility; allowing them to cope with strategy change, change in the competitive environment and in commercial priorities. The deal may need to be reshaped to accommodate this and the commercial structure must follow.

Objectives of the payment structure

Understanding the objectives of the payment structure is critical to choosing the right commercial solutions. The organisation's business goals will be the key source for these objectives. Explicitly stated, cost-oriented business goals, such as cost reduction, will be simple to identify and easy to integrate into the commercial solution. But, every business goal should be examined, as many of the goals may yield underlying payment objectives that will shape the overall payment structure.

For example, if an organisation is seeking stability as a key goal as well as cost reduction, then achieving certainty in the payment structure will drive the overall objective of the commercial solution. Aligning business goals with payment objectives is outcome-driven and there are three general themes to consider: demand-driven payments that vary in line with the fluctuations in the business; achieving certainty through a high degree of definitiveness and regularity of payments; and reaping the benefits of transformational change without incurring additional up-front spend.

The demand-driven model closely aligns payments with the peaks and troughs of the business, with payments going up and down according to agreed parameters (see Figure 3.12). Such approaches are particularly suitable for organisations wishing to correspond paying for services with the patterns of the business, for example the volatility of travel ticket processing. Common implementations of demand driven pricing are transaction-based and resource-based mechanisms.

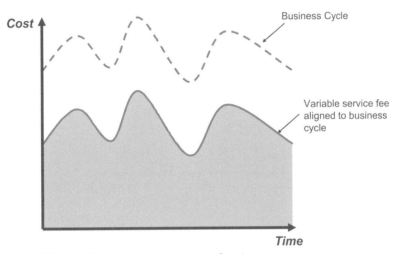

Figure 3.12 Demand-driven payment mechanism

Selecting the right demand-driven payment mechanism is dependent on three factors: the amount of risk the client wishes to transfer to the supplier; the period of commitment for the outsourcing arrangement; and the ownership of resource control. For example, transaction-based pricing transfers a large element of risk to the supplier and often requires a long-term commitment from the client. For resource-based pricing, clients have the ability to flex resources without the need for a long-term commitment; however the risk of success primarily remains with the client.

Certainty is a payment objective directed at achieving stability and regularity in the service payments. This can either be at a steady level for a fixed budget, or at a controlled increase or decrease in line with expected business expansion or contraction. This approach introduces steadiness for organisations that require their outsourced service function as an entity with a known recurring fee. Fixed-price payment mechanisms are the most common implementations of this approach and are often associated with stringent service level agreements (see Figure 3.13).

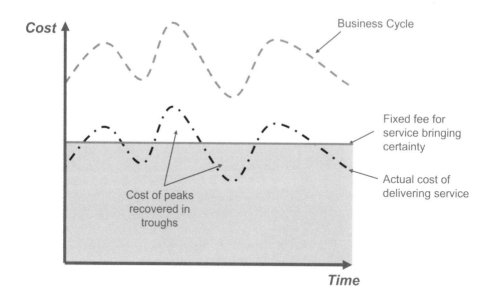

Figure 3.13 Certainty payment mechanism

During service peaks, suppliers would bear any additional costs and recover these costs during low periods of service demand. Suppliers would normally expect a medium- to long-term commitment in order to accommodate the recovery of these additional peak costs. Clients can also benefit from steady year-on-year cost reductions within a fixed-price mechanism by tuning the payment profile, either by reducing the scope of service or by supplier-initiated productivity improvements.

A transformational payment objective allows organisations to benefit from front-loaded investment programmes by smoothing out costs during the subsequent ongoing service period. With this payment objective, the supplier bears a large amount of risk, as it funds up-front investments and recovers these costs by applying an appropriate margin on the cost of providing the ongoing service (see Figure 3.14). Throughout the service period the client has the major advantage of paying the same fixed fee. Consequently, many suppliers seek a long-term commitment to secure a suitable period for recovering the initial investment.

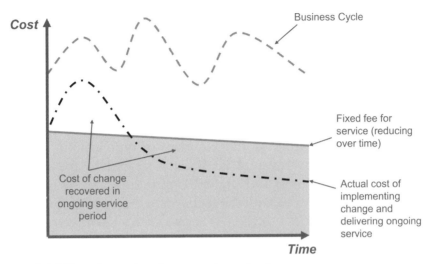

Figure 3.14 Transformational payment mechanism

Payment structures: tools and techniques

Traditionally organisations considering outsourcing payment options had little choice and the scope for creativity was limited. Arrangements centred on a singular approach, usually a time and materials or fixed-price basis. This was satisfactory for simply constructed deals with basic payment objectives such as low-cost access to skills or service cost reduction.

With outsourcing becoming a driver for business agility – rather than purely a cost-cutting measure – other, more sophisticated mechanisms have materialised. Choosing the right commercial solutions has evolved into using one or more payment structures to meet the payment objectives. The choice of tools and techniques is extensive and ever changing, but solutions derive from three core elements: basic structures; risk and reward structures; and financial and leasing options.

Traditionally, outsourcing offered four basic payment structures: time and materials; fixed price; open book or cost plus; and joint ventures. The mainstay of many deals remains time and materials or fixed price, while the appetite for open book or cost plus and joint ventures has reduced in recent years, owing to their complexity and the need for additional costs when establishing and servicing such arrangements.

The time and materials model

Using a time and materials model, clients purchase resources or skills on an as-needed basis to an agreed rate card. Normally, there is no commitment to achieving service levels by the supplier as both the strategic and operational control remains with the client. This allows a high degree of flexibility and control for the client, but does not enable the supplier to bring in efficiencies through economies of scale or shared resources. Neither is the supplier incentivised to introduce productivity gains, as revenue is directly related to the use of its resources. However, time and materials structure can be used effectively for low-risk services with the focus on resource availability rather than service levels, or as a means to access *ad hoc* resource capacity.

The fixed-price approach

In a fixed-price approach, suppliers commit to delivering the service for a set fee. The fee can be constant or increasing and decreasing within defined parameters. Fixed-price allows clients consistency and regularity in the cost base, coupled with delivery to known levels of services. Service level agreements (SLAs) are essential for fixed-price structures and both client and supplier need to ensure that SLAs are achievable and do not constrain the service unnecessarily. A high proportion of risk is transferred to the supplier, as the responsibility for achieving SLAs is placed on a contractual footing. This approach incentivises the supplier to introduce productivity improvements to enhance the quality of service, as this will increase the margin on the deal.

Open book or cost-plus plans

Open book or cost-plus plans require the client to pay for the service on the basis of the actual cost with the addition of an agreed margin. While this structure shares risk between the client and supplier, it does shift the emphasis of service delivery from service to financial. A feature of this approach is that clients gain granular access to financial details, allowing the ability to exert a high level of management over the cost-base. However, this can become disadvantageous for the outsourcing relationship, especially if the supplier's flexibility is curtailed as a consequence.

Further, there is little incentive for suppliers to introduce productivity initiatives, such as using shared resources, as they may dilute their margin on the deal. Indeed, the advantage of lower-cost access to shared resources may not actually be available as this could reveal confidential cost information of other clients using the same resources. Both parties may incur further costs by employing additional effort to closely scrutinise financial aspects of all elements of the service.

Joint ventures

Joint ventures require the client and supplier to establish a special-purpose vehicle to provide the outsourcing service. This can range from straightforward contractual partnerships through to equity investment ventures including collaborative acquisition. This type of structure offers a true partnership approach and can act as a half-way house to full transfer outsourcing. All parties share the risk within a joint venture and they also share the rewards, as elements of the joint venture tend to be ring-fenced for the purpose of service.

A joint venture arrangement can be considered for specialist outsourcing services that can be replicated for other clients. For example, a pharmaceutical company could work with an outsourcing supplier to establish a business processing service for its human resources function. A profitable venture could then be created by offering these services to other pharmaceutical organisations.

But there are many issues for both sides within joint ventures. They can be difficult to establish and it can be hard to gain approval from executive boards and shareholders. Additional investment is usually required to prepare and manage financial and legal aspects, and joint ventures do have the potential to create conflicts in areas such as management and intellectual property.

Risk and reward structures

The primary objective of risk and reward payment structures is to balance the sharing of risk within the service with an appropriate incentive scheme. There are many types of risk and reward payment structures, with each offering the ability to apportion different levels of risk with corresponding rewards for success and penalties for failure. Such payment structures can overlay basic payment structures to create the right commercial solution, and risk and reward payment structures commonly include: service credits and bonuses; capping and gain sharing; benefits-based pricing; transaction-based pricing; and budget management pricing.

Service credits and bonuses

Service credits and bonuses can be used to influence the behaviour of a supplier by penalising under-achievement and rewarding over-achievement. Delivery to SLAs for the agreed fee is a given for suppliers, but failure to meet an SLA will entitle the client to a monetary or time-based credit. Similarly, if the supplier performs better than the SLA, the client agrees to pay a bonus over and above the normal service fee. Clients should take care when using service bonuses as if they become too regular, this could point to inappropriate or lenient SLAs.

Service credits are most effective when used as a sharp stick against the supplier, rather than as a sledgehammer. High credit values may seem good deterrents, but insisting on very large credits may adversely affect the supplier and, possibly, its ability to deliver the service.

Capping

Capping is commonly used with time and material mechanisms to protect the client from cost productivity overruns by applying a limit to the service fee. In time and materials based services, where fees can be variable, capping assures clients that the fees will never exceed a predefined limit.

Gain sharing

Gain sharing is commonly applied to fixed-price services, where any productivity improvements that may result in a lower service cost are passed on to the client, usually as a lower fee, partially or wholly related to the decrease. The service fee will never exceed the fixed-price agreements, but has the potential to reduce in line with service improvements. This may discourage suppliers from introducing productivity improvements, as the sharing could diminish their financial gain.

Benefits-based pricing

Benefits-based pricing shapes the payment structure by attributing payments to key achievements. Examples could be improved end-user response times for an application, or reduction in debtor days for a financial business processing service. This approach encourages the supplier to introduce service innovations to ensure the client fully realises the benefits from outsourcing. Critical to using benefits-based pricing is collaboratively defining and articulating the measurement criteria. Additionally, the more risk a client expects a supplier to accept, the more the supplier will want to influence the end-to-end business service.

Transaction-based pricing

Transaction-based pricing offers the client the ability to link service payments with business patterns. This is particularly attractive to client organisations wishing to profile their payments in accordance with their business throughput. While the supplier bears a large amount of risk and makes potentially significant investment costs, it can gain substantially from higher demands for the service. Additionally, any margin improvements gained through productivity initiatives are normally retained by the supplier.

The transaction-based pricing mechanisms require a high level of scrutiny during set-up, as well as during ongoing periods. Suppliers tend to require an extensive study of the client's business model in order to develop a sound business plan for the outsourcing service. Critical within this business plan is a comprehensive understanding of the relationship between business revenue and the cost-base of the service – a misalignment could prove detrimental to the outsourcing supplier leading to difficulties in providing the service.

Transaction-based pricing has been used successfully for high-volume business, such as travel ticketing, where both client and supplier can fully engage at all levels – strategic through to operational.

Budget management pricing

Budget management pricing is an enabler for a transformational payment objective. The supplier commits to delivering a service to the client's budget and may also include the prospect of reducing the fee over time. Changes or one-off investment programmes are funded by the supplier, with any incurred costs recovered during the ongoing service. In other words, a smoothing-out profile. The client benefits from retaining a high level of certainty regarding the payment fee, while having the added advantage of receiving changes to the service.

As the nature of this payment structure means that suppliers are funding investments in the service, their financial exposure is much greater, especially for cash flow management. Therefore, a long-term commitment by the client would normally be expected to ensure a sufficient time period to recover any investments. A further incentive for suppliers is the possibility of retaining the financial benefits of productivity introduced into the outsourcing service.

Budget management pricing can be very attractive to clients intending to use outsourcing as an instrument for change. Its success does rely on all parties agreeing to a mutually beneficial financial profile built on an accurate and properly constructed contract.

Choice and implementation

Choosing and implementing the right payment structure is not easy, as both client and supplier have to balance commercial interests with business risk (see Figure 3.15). Getting the best terms is an important goal for both sides, but it is imperative that the final solution is beneficial to the client's business, from a financial and service perspective. For example, if a client achieves stringent financial arrangements mostly balanced in its favour, this may have constraining consequences on the ability of the supplier to deliver effectively.

Every outsourcing agreement is unique, but there are some common pointers to consider when developing the right commercial model:

- Align to goals – the payment structure must incentivise all parties to behave in a manner that is aligned to the client's business goals

- Apportion risk with appropriate rewards – the level of risk being shared must be clear, with the commercial solution accommodating a suitable reward structure

- Balance control and empowerment – the right payment structure will reflect the level of control over the service by both client and supplier

- Simple to understand and implement – complex and intricate payment structures can become unwieldy to use. Strive for a transparent solution that is easy to measure and simple to administer

- Flexibility to adapt – change to the outsourcing service is inevitable, either directly or indirectly. The commercial solution must have an element of flexibility to accommodate business change without instigating major contractual change

- Allow suppliers to turn profit – profitable gain from outsourcing encourages suppliers to engender a collaborative working approach, creating an environment where the emphasis is on business benefit rather than purely on cost.

Figure 3.15 Pointers to a successful commercial approach

3.5

Effective Governance

Building a partnership

When a client and supplier enter into an outsourcing agreement, they automatically begin a relationship. The origin of this relationship will be drawn from the commercial structure and contractual details. To advance from an embryonic relationship through to a successful partnership can be a difficult path to follow, particularly if outsourcing is a new corporate direction.

Success is achieved where both sides are aligned to the same goals. Understanding each other and how best to work together becomes easier to articulate when client and supplier subscribe to a common approach for developing and managing their relationship.

Governing relationships

There are many ways a relationship can be governed. Irrespective of size, scope and complexity of contract, some form of governance will always be needed. Whatever approach is deployed, there are three crucial areas at the core of effective governance: the goals of the relationship, an appropriate working framework, and the principles for operating.

Successful governance involves:

- clear and aligned goals;

- clarity of approach;

- compatibility between the outsourcing approach and governance approach; and

- unambiguous roles and responsibilities that provide clear empowerment and accountability.

There is no silver bullet to governance, as the approach is based on the many variables of the undertaking. However, it must fit the commercial structure and be tailored specifically for the sensitivities of the deal. By defining the goals of the relationship as opposed to just the goals of the service, a charter can be laid out that specifies what is included and excluded from the relationship. Flexibility can be introduced by outlining degrees of freedom within these defined boundaries. The principles of partnership and collaboration will form the thrust of the goals, with every client and supplier engagement having specific targets according to the details of the engagement.

The goals must also be mapped onto the type of outsourcing service being employed, be it conventional, problem-solving or transformational. This provides a means for both client and supplier to shape the necessary models, structures and processes to effectively govern the relationship.

The traditional concept of approaching a relationship saying, 'I'm paying, so you do as I say', may feel right in terms of retaining control, but it does not encourage a collaborative working environment. There are alternatives, especially for those seeking to use the relationship as a collective, positive influence for the service. The final approach will be dependent on the overall objectives of using outsourcing and can be a blend of different themes (see Figure 3.16).

Designing and implementing a suitable approach is a natural continuation of the outsourcing procurement and implementation process. The chosen themes must be combined with attributes of the outsourcing arrangement. These can be derived from the outsourcing strategy supplier proposition documents and contract agreements that include:

- objectives and reasoning for outsourcing;

- expectations of the service;

- commercial incentive structure and the obligations of all parties.

Theme	Direction
Innovate and improve	Governance actions that are creative with value added as a prominent influence.
Business value-based	Clear understanding of the value that governance actions bring to the client's business, often with client and supplier jointly agreeing the justifications.
Master or servant	The client occupies the master role and the suppliers occupy a servant role. The client leads and directs with little influence from the supplier.
Safe pair of hands	Any action has a high degree of risk containment, with both sides taking a cautious approach. Risk exposure is minimised; however this can be to the detriment of creativity and innovation.
Cost containment	Any action has to minimise expenditure, with the key focus on achieving goals by restraining cost. This can have a constraining impact on investment and development of the service.
Exception driven	Governance gives priority to progressing escalation matters. This devolves a high degree of autonomy to the supplier and client delivery units with little combined strategic guidance.

Figure 3.16 Themes for governing relationships

Types of outsourcing agreement

Most outsourcing agreements can be categorised as traditional, problem-solving or transformational. The level of collaboration increases from a conventional to a transformational arrangement and the approach to managing relationships will differ (see Figure 3.17).

The main focus of a traditional outsourcing service tends to be operational and entails transferring a well-run operation to a specialist supplier. The objective is to maintain the service within the service level agreements (SLAs) while reducing costs. A primary goal of the relationship within this type of outsourcing will be to ensure that the service is provided optimally for the client's core business to function efficiently. Therefore, the approach to governance will lean towards being SLA driven, with elements such as cost containment and exception only being key influences.

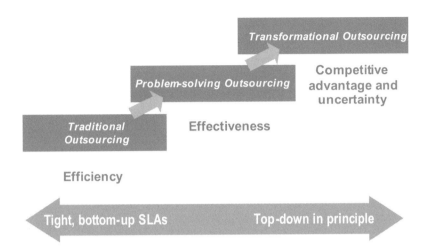

Figure 3.17 Match the relationship with the objectives

For problem-solving outsourcing services, the emphasis tends to be tactical. This type of outsourcing builds on traditional outsourcing with variations that cater for key tactical issues that a client needs to address. For example, clearing major backlogs of problems or stabilising a particularly problematic IT or business processing service. The goals of the relationship will include those normally defined within traditional outsourcing as well as specific objectives for the tactical issues. Therefore, the governance approach will be SLA driven with the additional influences of innovation and improvement.

Transformational outsourcing services tend to be strategic, with the focus on using outsourcing as a catalyst for organisational change, so the goals are fundamentally different to other forms of outsourcing. Supplier and client need to work hand-in-hand to ensure the undertaking achieves the core change, not just the SLA. The resulting governance is a complex combination of innovation and improvement, business value and operational service targets.

Building a governance model

While every outsourcing agreement is unique, there are six attributes for a successful approach to developing and managing a thriving relationship. These are:

- building the relationship on common top-down and aligned goals;

- having a clear structure with understood roles;

- enabling participative governance at all levels of the relationship;

- being open and clear in communication with no surprises;

- encouraging collaborative creativity; and

- striving to achieve a genuine partnership through effective governance.

Organisations need to have the flexibility to change direction in order to meet the dynamic demands of their markets. This, in turn, means that the details of an outsourcing arrangement will inevitably be subject to change over time. Consequently, jointly agreed top-down and aligned goals that are appropriately incentivised will be critical in order to succeed. Being able to flex and respond to new requirements is always challenging and success relies on all parties having a clear, long-term view of where the organisation as a whole is heading.

Once an outsourcing contract has been agreed, clients and suppliers immediately focus on implementing the agreement. In the lead-up to the start of the service, there are a range of activities to transfer ownership. It is during this build up that it is essential to clearly define and agree a structure to manage and steer the ongoing delivery of services. This structure is known as a governance model and its successful implementation hinges on mutual agreement, clarity and simplicity.

The governance model is the blueprint for the management of the outsource. It provides clear guidance for all those concerned with the service, rather than acting as a forum for senior executives. Ideally, the model should have a maximum of three tiers: supervisory, management, and operational (see figure 3.18).

All parties involved in any outsourcing arrangement are jointly responsible for the results across the entire period of the contract. Once a governance model is defined, agreed and implemented, it needs to be held up as 'the way we work', and must be genuinely relevant to everyone. The relationships between the teams of people involved in the detail of the operation are crucial. Both client and supplier must encourage all staff to participate in the spirit of partnership.

Supervisory Tier	Board to Board					
	Joint Partnership Board					
Management Tier	Strategic Management	Portfolio Management	Performance Management	Financial Management	Commercial Management	Business Change Management
Operational Tier	Service Delivery Management					

The supervisory tier is where business strategies are aligned and directions are set. This tier sets the framework for and the tone of the partnership. It manages conflicting demands and mobilises responses to issues arising outside the boundaries of the partnership. Where issues cannot be resolved at the operational or managerial level, then the supervisory tier takes responsibility for resolution.

The management tier is where the senior managers responsible for delivering each of the component parts of the service will form a management team. The actual number of component parts depends on the size and complexity of the outsourcing service. Nonetheless, management responsibility must be clearly defined, even for those parts that have a minor role. This tier has the crucial purpose of implementing the strategies and goals jointly defined in the supervisory tier.

The operational tier is aimed at ensuring that day to day service is robust and cohesive across all aspects of the service. This is achieved by underpinning the entire service with common service delivery management processes, practices and toolsets. As a result, all parties are enabled to transact the business of delivering the outsourced services smoothly.

It is important that individuals within the service have a clear understanding of their roles and responsibilities across all tiers.

Figure 3.18 Example governance model

Effective communication is a critical enabler for a successful relationship; it must be frequent and relevant. For example, does the process focus on confrontational monthly bashings or on daily solution-developing meetings?

The concept of openness can be difficult to implement in a contractual environment. However, a clear governance model with joint goals and objectives builds mutual respect and trust. Openness is particularly important when problems occur with the service. Both parties should have the confidence to provide early notification of issues and suggested resolution steps, rather than retrenching into defensive positions.

Strong communications will increase the ability to adapt to requirements as they change. A weak relationship with lower levels of responsiveness, reliability and communication can create an imbalanced partnership, epitomised by caution and distrust.

Both partners in an outsourcing relationship bring unique skills and capabilities to the service. Many suppliers of outsourcing services have developed a wide variety of experiences through dealing with clients across the spectrum of industries, whilst clients have a deep level of understanding of their own business and are usually seeking partners to help them innovate.

By bringing together these differing perspectives, creativity can flourish for the benefit of the client's business. This can be achieved by implementing an effective governance approach that brings together partnership, trust and common goals as a platform for developing innovative solutions. For this to work, both partners must be prepared to be creative and to draw on the best experience they bring. Governance structures must not restrict innovation, they should seek to enable it (see Figures 3.19 and 3.20).

The ultimate aim of any outsourcing relationship has to be to create a level of trust and confidence that moves the supplier interaction from a stagnant, 'you wanted to do this. Here's the technology or approach that can make it happen', to a more creative 'we've been looking at the way you do business and listened to your concerns. Have you thought about doing it in this completely different way with this new piece of technology or service? The benefits are x, the costs are y and the risks are z. If you wish, we can take you to a site where this is working. And also, here's a prototype of how it may look and feel'.

Do

- *Understand your type of outsourcing and define your goals for the relationship*
- *Agree on a strategy for implementing governance*
- *Define a clear and simple governance model including roles and responsibilities*
- *Engage early with suppliers to ensure governance is ready from day one of the service*
- *Change the governance approach to meet the changes in the business*
- *Be firm but fair; if suppliers default then penalise if necessary, but move on once the problem has been cleared*
- *Treat outsourcing as an investment and use governance to manage that investment.*

Don't

- *Use governance as a supplier bashing tool; it will only promote confrontation and defensiveness*
- *Be rigid in the model, build in flexibility*
- *Treat governance as exclusive to senior executives; everyone is part of the process*
- *Approach governance as 'one size fits all'; use goals to determine the best approach for each outsourcing arrangement.*

Figure 3.19 Do's and don'ts of governance

- *Mutual understanding of goals for the relationship*
- *Simple and clear governance model*
- *Clarity in roles and responsibilities*
- *Open and honest two-way communications*
- *An environment in which innovative and stimulating solutions develop for the common cause.*

Figure 3.20 Factors for achieving excellence in governance

3.6

The Human Side of Outsourcing

Best practices for successful outsourcing

In the present economic climate, many companies are turning to outsourcing, often using low-cost offshore locations, in order to boost efficiencies and reduce costs.

There is a perception that doing this results in a harmful outcome for employees. Instead, there are upsides and downsides. Typically, cost reduction involves an element of reducing overheads, and transferring staff costs to a service provider is one way of doing this. What this means for staff varies depending on a number of factors, including the geographic location of existing and future services.

A survey conducted by Capgemini highlights the fact that few employees understand the implications of outsourcing to them personally, or know what questions they need to ask in this situation.

Endgames for employees

There is no single answer to the issue of human resources, but there are four possible endgames for employees. The final solution will usually involve a blend of these and will be largely driven by the objectives of the outsource and the shape of the proposed solution.

The choices are between whether employees stay with their current employer or move to the outsourcer, and whether they continue to use their current skill-set or are retrained and moved into other roles (see Figure 3.21).

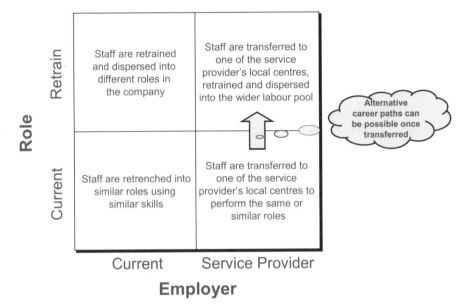

Figure 3.21 Outcomes for employees

The least disruptive endgame for employees is to be trained and moved into other roles within their current company. They are guaranteed to keep their terms, conditions and culture, and are retrained with new skills. For small numbers this is a feasible option, but for larger numbers it is often not possible, and, in this situation, temporary contracts are usually terminated.

Alternatively, employees could transfer to other departments within their current company and use their current skills. This is very unlikely to be a large-scale endgame as many jobs are specific to a process or function and there would not be vacant jobs requiring the same skills. However, employers normally look to keep a proportion of organisational knowledge and skills, so an element of this option can be possible, with staff experiencing very little disruption.

A third scenario sees employees transferred to the service provider and continuing to perform the same role, delivering the same service. This is the most typical scenario for outsourcing agreements. Employees continue their contracts of employment with the outsourcer from the point of transfer. This does depend on location and how the future service will be delivered. In this situation, outsourcers try to keep service delivery within a suitable commuting area, enabling current staff to continue their roles. In this endgame, staff are transferred into the service provider's company under protected transfer and keep their employment status, terms and conditions.

Because outsourcing companies are never static and deliver services to multiple companies, employees essentially join a more diverse labour pool where their skills and experience can be used in other parts of the business. In many cases this opens up career opportunities that were not previously available. There are many success stories of transferred people reaching senior management levels within the outsourcing company. However, career progression is not the only measure of success; career development and depth of expertise are also measures of success.

Conversely, where services are delivered from different geographies, service providers increasingly have centres that are already staffed, and they are too far to commute to or are culturally too different. The result is that redundant roles are terminated.

A final alternative is for employees to be transferred to the service provider, retrained and dispersed into other parts of the supplier business. This is only viable if the service provider has a structure where it can retrench the staff to other jobs. For many suppliers this is not the case, as their shared delivery centres are already staffed. If this move can be made, staff continue their current contracts of employment under transfer under protected employment (TUPE) terms (see Figure 3.24), and, depending on location, may need to commute or relocate to be near the outsourcer's offices. Such a change may not be attractive to all employees in the transfer, but, where possible, employees gain new skills and are exposed to a broader scope of careers and opportunities.

One essential for success of the staff transfer is accurately matching grades between the two companies. Staff who are accurately graded will be better positioned to contribute effectively to the business. Redundancy is the least constructive scenario for both employer and employees. Employers and suppliers must use economic, technical or organisational reasons to justify headcount reductions as part of the outsource. Redundancies simply as a result of outsourcing are not allowed under TUPE, resulting in up-front redundancy costs and delays to the cost savings from outsourcing.

Protection against redundancy

For employees, this outcome is unsettling. The shape of the outsourcing solution means it is not feasible for them to transfer or be retrained. Permanent and fixed-term contract staff are protected by TUPE through redundancies, providing a legal framework to ensure employees are given due notice to prepare and unions and workers' councils are consulted to negotiate exit terms and packages. In business transfers, fixed-term contractors and permanent employees are eligible for transfer under protected employment, through TUPE. This protects employment status, terms and conditions, although it currently excludes normal retirement pension terms.

The case for temporary contractors is slightly different, as they can only claim unfair dismissal after 12 months' service, and are only entitled to redundancy after two years' service. However, because most transfers involve a percentage of contract staff, many service providers choose to renew temporary contracts for an initial period as this is the most effective way of protecting against a loss of key knowledge and ensuring service level continuity. At the end of this period, and depending on the needs of the business, contractors are offered either a contract renewal or permanent positions within the service provider, or their contracts are terminated in accordance with their terms.

Good practice in staff transfer

There are many reports highlighting how motivated workforces deliver higher productivity, making it clear that an acknowledged policy on human resources is essential in any business transfer. Providing information, contact and reassurance to employees will sustain motivation and morale to preserve service levels, but failure to address employee questions and concerns can disrupt service delivery both during transition and beyond.

This is a time of change when employees feel vulnerable and uninformed. Good practice involves implementing a comprehensive communication and involvement programme to ensure that employees are part of the transition process and have active support.

A high-level process designed to engage staff throughout the transition process and onwards should be implemented as soon as employees are informed by their company of the intention to transfer them and their jobs under a business transfer agreement (see Figure 3.22).

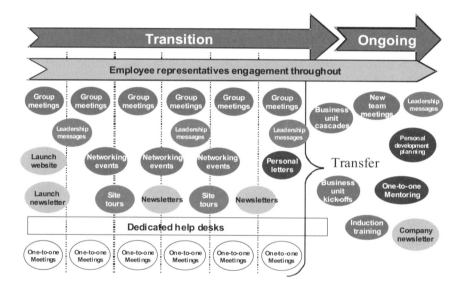

Figure 3.22 Transition of staff during business transfer

The aim of the process is to prevent disruption to the business by welcoming and reassuring employees, and, on a continuing basis, to update them on progress, involve them and their representatives, answer questions and seek feedback. Employees will be motivated to maintain or increase productivity if they understand that their future is safe. It is important to provide clear information on individual employment rights, the process of transfer, the new employer's policies and culture, and the way ahead for transferring employees.

Messages that must be delivered to employees include: information about the outsourcer, such as background, the position of the transferred employees within the company, career and training opportunities within the company, and the effects on terms and conditions and pensions. Also required are information about the transfer, such as the scope of the business transfer, how the transfer will work and when it will begin, and what the service from the outsourcer looks like.

To deliver this information, a variety of events and contacts will be necessary, with the sort of participative activities to which employees should have exposure, including: meetings and mentoring, networking events, training and site tours, and access to newsletters and websites.

Roadshow presentations can give a short introduction to the new company and culture, confirming the process and what changes the transfer will bring. Personal one-to-one discussion should be available to all employees to address any individual concerns they may have.

This is also an opportunity for the transition team to get to know and understand the local issues that are important to employees, seek the views of individuals on the way ahead and establish individual employees' aspirations and career aims. In particular, conducting a number of pension seminars to explain the pension schemes and options available helps employees feel more at ease.

Visits to the new employer's premises to sample daily working life and meet new colleagues, many of whom will have been through the TUPE process themselves, is valuable for creating a more positive environment. Undertaking regular formal consultation with employee representatives, including recognised trade unions, also helps to smooth the transition and reassure all involved that the transfer is a positive step.

Communication and the highest possible level of transparency is essential to the transfer process. To remain productive, employees need to have information that will answer their immediate questions. The prospect of outsourcing can be daunting and although employees have a number of questions, they are often not sure what questions to raise (see Figure 3.23).

These questions and answers are as critical as all the other human resources issues pertaining to outsourcing (see Figure 3.25). Ultimately, it is people that make business successful and it is in everyone's interests to get this part of the process right.

What will happen to my terms and conditions?

Under protected transfer, terms and conditions are matched to the same or equivalent terms and conditions with the new employer. In many cases there will be little recognisable change. Often, once the transferred employees have settled into their new employer's organisation for a number of months, they are offered corresponding terms and conditions which are standard for the outsourcing company. This is done so that there is parity of benefits, it promotes equity and develops a sense of belonging to further reassure those who have transferred. The only caveat is around the terms of normal company retirement pensions. They are not protected under TUPE and are for workers' councils or unions to negotiate on behalf of employees.

What support networks are available for people who join the company through an outsourcing route?

Outsourcing companies have well-established support networks and professional human resources teams that induct and manage new employees into the company. The communications and involvement processes that are used during transition ensure that all transferees are informed and have the opportunity to express concerns both during and after transition.

What career opportunities will be open to me?

Outsourcing organisations offer a variety of careers and skills diversification, more so because they provide a range of business and IT services to multiple customers. They support employee careers with regular counselling, where the objective is to provide each individual with the means to create an actionable personal development plan, describing their aspirations and the training and experience they need to achieve these.

What learning and development opportunities will be on offer to me?

In order for outsourcing businesses to grow, employers need to develop an organisation that is continually updated with new skills, knowledge and experience. In short, they must maintain existing skills and develop new ones. For this reason, they are committed to comprehensive employee development programmes that are both participative and systematic.

How will the transfer happen?

Normally, the transfer is a three-stage process. First, the employees are provided with information about the transfer, including information about the reasons for the outsource, the outsourcing company and what it means for the employees. Second, employees are invited to make site visits, meet with future colleagues and get to know and be welcomed by their new employer. Third, any scheduled physical moves takes place. This can be phased prior to contract date, to ensure that service delivery is not overly exposed to risk and is proven to work. It results in a gradual physical move of all employees to fully deliver services from the new location within the transfer deadline. However this is not always the case, and services may continue to be delivered from the existing physical location.

Are there any differences in the way you treat people who join the company as a result of an outsourcing deal?

Leading outsourcing companies do not distinguish between existing employees and those being transferred, they seek to create open and collaborative environments that are well motivated and deliver high productivity. Treating employees that transfer into their environment differently would counter this objective and lower the ability to leverage skills and experience across multiple customers.

Figure 3.23 Common employee questions

The UK Transfer of Undertakings (Protection of Employment) Regulations 1981 (known as 'TUPE') were originally introduced in order to implement the EC Acquired Rights Directive, adopted in 1977. Designed to protect both the employer and employee during business transfers, it provides a legal framework to ensure that both parties are treated and act fairly.

For an employee who transfers to a new employer as a result of a business transfer, TUPE protects the employee's contract of employment. The employee transfers on the same terms and conditions that existed prior to the transfer, including such matters as pay and annual leave entitlements.

It also ensures that the employee's service with the former employer is fully recognised. Any collective agreements made by a recognised union on behalf of the employee shall have effect as if made by or on behalf of the new employer.

For the employer, this means a set of rules for the transfer to the new supplier. However it does not bypass needing to negotiate staff terms and conditions with the supplier, or the possibility of recrimination from staff being transferred.

Currently, the main exclusions from protection under TUPE are terms that relate to an occupational pension scheme. Normally, a recognised union or workers council negotiates these terms.

Figure 3.24 Protection of employee rights – Transfers of Undertakings (Protection of Employment)

Capgemini's survey of UK-based employees' perceptions of outsourcing identified:

☐ *Awareness of the outsourcing concept is high, employees understand its main benefits for the organisation and why it is an option often chosen by employers.*

☐ *Most people appreciate the potential benefits of outsourcing for themselves personally, with factors such as better career opportunities, higher pay, better working conditions, better training, development facilities and an enhanced CV being frequently quoted.*

☐ *Most people perceive a potential downside to outsourcing in terms of reduced job and pension security, increased workload, more stress and a forced move of work location.*

☐ *People have a poor understanding of their legal rights as employees if faced with the prospect of being outsourced and there is much confusion regarding sources of information and advice.*

Figure 3.25 Attitudes to outsourcing

3.7

Successful Transition

The moment of truth in service outsourcing

Successful transition is as pivotal to outsourcing as it is difficult. It can involve the transfer of knowledge, resources and assets from multiple geographic locations. It is distinct from delivery; the driver is a target date rather than service level agreement (SLA) and the cut-over to delivery deadline is normally immovable. Above all, transition lays the groundwork for the relationship and the future.

Transition is a 'moment of truth'. It is often the most disruptive period in the arrangement, with activities shifting from procurement into actual delivery. A poor start can comprise service and trust significantly, with far-reaching consequences for the relationship. Poor transition results in sub-optimal knowledge transfer and ill-defined responsibilities, adverse staff perceptions and morale, and a dip in service quality. It also puts a brake on the momentum of the relationship.

Offshore outsourcing complicates transition further. Geography and distance both impact the ability to transfer knowledge, and legal requirements can impact the speed at which outsourcing can take place.

Defining activity streams

A good approach includes clear and defined streams of activity and milestones. At a high level, the approach is often made up of three stages: understanding the starting point; building the future environment; and transferring the elements of the service (see Figure 3.26). Each stage has one or two phases of activity that build chronologically to reach the cut-over to delivery.

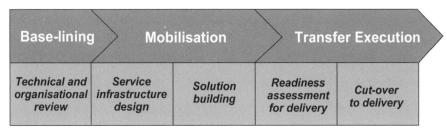

Figure 3.26 The three high-level stages of transition

Base-lining

In the initial stage, base-lining, there is one phase covering a technical and organisational review. The aim is to identify and document the service elements in scope – hardware, applications, people and so on – the knowledge base and environment used by the client. The results are reviewed with the client and actions to improve the service are agreed. Collaboration is important to ensure that accurate information is gathered during the exercise, as this will confirm the assumptions made during the early planning activities and ensure that the contract and associated schedules have a solid base. This phase normally includes base-lining both project development work and operational services.

Mobilisation

The second stage, mobilisation, has two phases. The first is service and infrastructure design. This defines the target service environment, making use of best practices. A plan is agreed to build the infrastructure and service components with the client in order to achieve the desired solution.

The second phase of mobilisation is solution building, when elements of the service are stabilised and controlled. Process changes to achieve best practices are also established and changes in supplier relationships are implemented. A plan to move to the target service environment is agreed and the required knowledge transfer is carried out.

A joint transition team between supplier and client is key to both these phases. This will enable best use of the business's services knowledge and the supplier's service transition experience. Working together, the partners can define the current service for each function or process in scope and prepare for the new supplier to assume responsibility through accelerated knowledge transfer.

One critical point is the definition of a clear knowledge transfer plan between any incumbent suppliers and the new supplier. There must be firm commitments and regular, formal communications to ensure progress to plan.

Transition execution

In the transition execution stage there are essentially two sub-phases. The first, readiness assessment for delivery, confirms which elements are in place to deliver the target services. Any outstanding work is planned and agreed with the business, while contractual terms are finalised and procedures agreed. In this phase service levels are also finalised and responsibilities agreed, the service quality plan is published and the knowledge transfer completed.

The second sub-phase, cut-over to delivery, transfers the service to the service provider. Any physical moves are executed and the new environment is formally accepted by the business. Additionally, the service teams that have been shadowing incumbent staff now become the technical teams and the service is delivered and measured against SLA targets that focus on key business priorities. Communicating with the business users to clarify and explain procedures and responsibilities is most important in this phase.

Second level activity streams

At the next level of detail and underpinning the three stages of transition, there are nine streams of activity and each is a contributor to one or more of the stages (see Figure 3.27).

	Base-lining		Mobilisation	Transfer Execution	
	Technical and organisational review	Service infrastructure design	Solution building	Readiness assessment for delivery	Cut-over to delivery
Technical aspects	X	X	X	X	X
Physical move			X		X
Service organisation and staff management	X	X	X		
Supplier management	X	X	X		
Financial and contractual aspects				X	
Procedure and documentation	X	X	X		
Knowledge transfer	X	X	X	X	
Estimating and planning	X	X			
Acceptance and sign-off	X	X		X	X

Figure 3.27 Activities underpinning the transition stage

The technical stream covers all the technical areas associated with the platform, applications, monitoring and support, including any infrastructure needed to run the service.

All the technical aspects of the current situation are reviewed and a technical target environment is designed and built. If any technical equipment is to be moved to the new supplier's premises, planning covers the move as well as tests before and after. A joint team of local technical experts and outsourcing solution architects to audit and develop the technical solution is advantageous.

The physical move is closely aligned to the technical stream. Some transitions require a physical move to the new supplier's premises which means human resources and transition teams need to work with the staff and asset owners during the course of the engagement. The move, if there is one, is then planned and completed, including equipment, infrastructure, furniture, people and any other assets.

The service organisation and staff management stream involves the process staff, management teams and IT support staff, and covers the human resources elements of transferring employees, and managing staff. The delivery organisation is developed, trained and implemented, and, if the new supplier takes over staff from the business, an induction is planned and performed. All personnel are then trained to meet the requirements of the new assignment.

Human resource governance is also initiated through this stream with service management routines such as billing and reporting being implemented. The current staff situation of the business is assessed and recommendations about possible recruitment are made to the new supplier's management. When the new supplier takes over personnel, some benefits, such as holidays, can be transferred.

Supplier management involves all third parties within the arrangement. A current supplier status is assessed in the review phase of the transition and contracts can be taken over by the new supplier or continue to be the responsibility of the business. At this point, new suppliers can also be contracted and old contracts can be terminated. Contractors' responsibilities are described and information about this is given to the business.

When it comes to financial and contractual aspects, the transition manager makes sure that all contractual aspects have been resolved before cut-over date. The sales process finalises contractual documents, but the transition manager may have to participate in the work. Service level agreements can be finalised in the transition, the sales process or the delivery phase depending on the organisational structure. If the service quality plan is to be formally accepted by the business, it might have to be handled as a contractual document. Finally, all billing procedures must be in place before cut-over date.

Procedures and documentation business staff should be involved in identifying existing process documentation and sharing knowledge. The current situation concerning documents and job schedules is assessed and all aspects of the future service delivery are documented. Similarly, business job schedules are transferred to the new supplier.

A balance must be reached between migrating service delivery to the new supplier's processes and practice, and retaining existing proven practices. The results of changing processes during transition may not deliver a step-change in performance, and the emotional effects of changing practices that have significant investment from existing staff could affect service quality and cause unnecessary disruption.

Knowledge transfer involves the business's staff and transition team working together to cover all actions that aim to transfer knowledge from the business to the new supplier. Knowledge within the new supplier should also be shared and documented, while tacit knowledge is also captured through shadowing staff and recording activities.

There will be systems or applications that have little documented knowledge, and risk assessment of these systems may show that they are not critical to the business. If this is the case, non-critical knowledge should be transferred, as appropriate, to achieve successful transition.

Some activities cannot be planned in detail in the original project plan because information from review and design phases is needed. However, time-critical activities must be planned and initiated by the transition team outside the process flow. For example, time and costs for any 'in-flight' programmes underway, such as planned system or application changes must be ascertained.

Ownership of such programmes requires an understanding of the impact they will have and how the service provider will work with the client to complete them. It is also necessary to estimate the impact and timescales of how they are transitioned if they are in the scope of the new arrangement.

The final piece of the jigsaw is acceptance and sign-off. The transition team needs to make sure that all acceptance and sign-off mechanisms are working smoothly, as a multitude of actions and results will be reviewed, accepted and signed-off by the business or the new supplier's management. Go and no-go decisions are made and documented, and all results need to be reviewed.

Finally, before start of delivery, all end-users must be informed about the new supplier's assignment and obligations, as well as their own.

Transition

Clearly transition is not just about the transfer of services. It is about making sure that services are set up for success and providing the best possible footing for them. Outsourcing involves change, and although services have been successfully transferred, the environments and people that were delivering services to agreed service levels have also changed. Features of offshore outsourcing are highlighted in Figure 3.28 and avoidance of the commoner pitfalls is addressed in Figure 3.29.

The post-transition period, often quoted as 90 days, is an opportunity for the supplier to firm up the delivery environment and, depending on the complexity of the service, retune the service to meet agreed service levels – the early stages of ongoing service delivery.

Post-transition is also when issues and concerns are addressed, and business benefits are measured to identify delivery shortfalls. The transition team, or elements of it, is still needed to follow through problems and action resolutions.

This period is particularly pertinent when outsourcing is carried out in a short time or services are transferred without change. Services can be consolidated and assets or headcounts reduced following the transfer of responsibility, although in complex cases the 90-day period is more usually used to stabilise the environment and plan for consolidation. In all cases, however, the focus must be on service delivery and maintaining service quality.

Offshore outsourcing is growing as countries including India, Poland and China offer significant cost savings in managing back-office and some front-office processes. The scope of services that can be delivered offshore is also increasing, adding to the complexity of transitioning.

Transition can take longer because of legislation that prevents rushed business transfers, while complexity is compounded by geography, language and distance of variants in the mix. Offshore transitions also carry the risk of failure to transfer knowledge when staff do not move with the service.

Creating local, smaller transition teams to prepare and execute transition from each country in the arrangement is a significant advantage to the offshore challenge. It enables a central, joint transition team to co-ordinate the overall service transfer remotely, running individual country transitions in parallel. This team can provide a central view of captured knowledge and minimise travel costs.

The alternative is to prepare a team that will migrate from country to country, transitioning services in phases. This serial approach takes longer, travel costs are higher and it may require a multilingual team capable of working closely with staff in each country.

Figure 3.28 Offshore variations

Transition is a complex period and with so many streams of activity the potential for problems is significant. Most stem from poor planning and communication, but there are lessons that can help avoid some of the pitfalls and set transition up for success.

Poor planning leads to ambiguity and can result in missing key elements of the transition. Understanding of the activities, dependencies and milestones of transition is essential, with the move most effectively managed in a series of steps. Clear planning, roles and responsibilities is a prerequisite for smooth transition. Before the start of the transition phase, a transition plan should be prepared, discussed and agreed between the business, new supplier, any incumbent suppliers and any other third parties. This plan will detail each activity and task to be completed, by whom and by when. It will also estimate the amount of effort required from both parties.

Infrequent and ambiguous communication can lead to misunderstandings and unnecessary barriers between the business, service staff and transition teams. To ensure confidence, particularly in a diverse and geographically dispersed environment, a communications programme can keep all parties up to date on what is happening, why, where and when.

The quality of service is dependent on the quality of knowledge retention. Knowledge is the foundation for continuity of services, and this ongoing improvement focusing on people, processes and technology ensures that knowledge is not only retained, but also becomes the foundation for future service success.

Collaboration between teams is essential to share skills, knowledge and experience and support the transfer of services. Joint transition teams should comprise new and current service providers, the business, customer representatives, industry and legal experts. It is critical for all stakeholders to have team members dedicated to the transition.

Figure 3.29 Avoiding pitfalls

Part Four

Case Histories

Introduction

Real experiences of benefiting from outsourcing

For over 30 years, Capgemini has been helping organisations use outsourcing as part of their corporate toolkit. Throughout this period there have been major revolutions and evolutions across the entire spectrum of commerce. Every aspect of doing business has been touched by many changes covering politics and government, technological innovation, business practice, market forces, as well as social and welfare. However for all organisations, there has been a constant need within all this change – the ability to adapt to change.

The case studies in this section are prime examples of how organisations have used outsourcing as a driver for adapting to change to meet specific business goals (see Table 4.1).

Table 4.1

Client	Country & Sector	Summary of Service	Client Quote	Key Capgemini Services
Britannic Assurance *IT Investment is springboard for success*	UK – Financial Services & Insurance	Transformation of IT into a customer-centric service by using a collaborative programme with Capgemini.	'We have been able to add vital new products to our portfolio, including the launch on-schedule of ISAs and Stakeholder Pensions, with total confidence in the new IT systems that support them.'	CRM, Support Services, Technology Consulting, Infrastructure Management, Business Process Management
CESPA *Transforms People Management processes via SAP-HR and backed by flexible Applications Management Services*	Spain – Energy & Utilities	Deploying SAP-HR with supporting processes and a flexible ongoing Applications Management service.	'We now have a base that allows us to face the future with new expectations for the development of Human Resources for our Group.'	Finance & Employee Transformation, Technology Consulting, EEA/ERP – SAP, Applications Management

Table 4-1 (cont'd)

Client	Country & Sector	Summary of Service	Client Quote	Key Capgemini Services
Coal Authority *Award-winning public service at lower cost using an innovative outsourcing contract, yielding major benefits*	UK – Energy & Utilities	Design, build and run a new Mining Reports and Surface Damage System under a Private Finance Initiative (PFI) arrangement.	'When we started we had mainframe systems, Cobol and Fortran systems. With the millennium issues about to come up, the Coal Authority didn't have the money to do the build or know-how to manage all the risks involved, so we put together the public finance initiative approach and used Capgemini, who understood the risks and the maturity of the business.'	Transformation Consulting, Systems Architecture, Applications Management, Infrastructure Management
Corus *Outsourced IT proves crucial to success of global business transformation*	UK – General Manufacturing	IT Transformation programme including a major outsourcing service for applications and infrastructure.	'Corus is undergoing a successful global transformation from a supplier of bulk steel tonnage to a provider of customer-driven solutions, and that change could not have taken place without the progress we have made in IT, assisted by outsourcing support to a world-class IT partner.'	Transformation Consulting, Applications Management, Infrastructure Management

Table 4-1 (cont'd)

Client	Country & Sector	Summary of Service	Client Quote	Key Capgemini Services
DARA *Fast Track towards an Adaptive Enterprise*	UK – Defence	Collaborative implementation of new business processes, applications and infrastructure.	'Outsourcing our IT to world-class professionals will also boost our ability to respond rapidly to whatever new needs may emerge in the fast-changing worlds of aviation and defence.'	Strategy Consulting, Supply Chain, AD & I Technology Consulting, Applications Management, Infrastructure Management, Business Process Management
Hydro One *Using outsourcing to adapt to market changes*	Canada – Energy & Utilities	Transformational outsourcing delivering comprehensive technology-enabled and business process management services.	'This arrangement with Capgemini will allow Hydro One to achieve cost saving and now focus on providing safe and reliable delivery of electricity at competitive prices.'	Transformation Consulting, Applications Management, Infrastructure Management, Business Process Outsourcing
GM Europe *Pan-European e-business websites linking GM across languages, cultures and business processes*	Europe – Automotive	Pan-European implementation and management of new applications and processes using a multinational 'partnership' team.	'…as a direct result of your team's efforts, GM Europe has taken a leadership position in deployment at eGM and is looked to as the example of "how to do it right"'!	B2B – Supply Chain, Infrastructure Management, Business Process Management, Technology Consulting

Table 4-1 (cont'd)

Client	Country & Sector	Summary of Service	Client Quote	Key Capgemini Services
Mercedes-Benz *Widening the window of confidence: comfort, style, performance, security and applications management services*	USA – Automotive	Flexible applications management, controlling costs and gaining access to additional skills.	'If it wasn't for the fact that Capgemini did the integration, we would have looked elsewhere for our AM support. The combination of integration and the "in-sourcing" met our expectations – that we will have a high level of quality support.'	Applications Management
Ontario Power Generation *Adaptive Outsourcing Solution via New Horizon Systems Solutions*	Canada – Energy & Utilities	A joint-venture outsourcing partnership to drive-down costs, increase quality and financially gain from offering specialist services to other organisations.	The direct result of this unique partnership with Capgemini is that we have divested about 65% of our operations, turned a huge technology cost into a new revenue stream, and still saved about 20% in IT costs.'	Strategy Consulting, Technology Consulting, Applications Management, Infrastructure Management, Business Process Management, Transformational Outsourcing

Table 4-1 (cont'd)

Client	Country & Sector	Summary of Service	Client Quote	Key Capgemini Services
Prudential *IT outsourcing gives flexibility and cost savings*	UK – Financial Services & Insurance	IT outsourcing of a data centre, associated services and staff to reduce operational costs and increase quality of service.	'The contract with Capgemini secures the flexibility of cost that is vital when operating in an environment that changes as rapidly as financial services. Fixed costs have been converted into variable costs and Prudential is now free to explore product and service innovations with the right level of IT support and expenditure.'	Applications Management, Infrastructure Management
Sprint *Expanding leadership through Applications Management outsourcing*	USA – Telecommunications	Applications management service, including dedicated Application Development Centres releasing Sprint to focus on their core competences.	'The project had a very aggressive schedule and challenging requirements. Capgemini stepped up to the challenge and met or exceeded all of the deadlines.'	Applications Management

Note: Infrastructure Management includes one or more of Data Centre Services, Network & Security Services and Desktop & Distributed Services.

Britannic Assurance

IT investment is springboard for success at Britannic Assurance

UK financial services company Britannic Assurance had ambitious plans for the future, with new business, new products and new channels-to-market all firmly in prospect. In consequence, the company needed to develop a modern systems infrastructure, powerful and flexible enough to support the considerable expansion and change that was planned.

Capgemini was chosen as main IT partner and, today, after a major investment in technology, the new systems are in place and proving a springboard for success. They are supporting new products and channels while facilitating improved efficiency, better customer focus, stronger management control and new cost savings.

Client profile

Britannic Assurance is a key part of the UK's Britannic Group, a modern financial services group offering optimal solutions to the requirements of its more than 1.5 million customers. The Group manages some £20 billion of funds, offers a broad spectrum of savings, insurance and investment products and has a solid 135-year history.

Britannic Assurance has for the past three years pursued an ambitious change programme with the strategic objective of becoming a modern, broadly-based financial services player, performance-driven and customer-focused. There has been a new emphasis on expansion, both by acquisition and organically, including diversification into new products and new channels to market.

Business issues

At the start of its change programme, Britannic Assurance faced some serious challenges arising from a huge transformation in the UK's financial services landscape. Deregulation and globalisation had brought many new competitors into the Group's traditional markets, and its customers were being bombarded by advertising messages from established players and new kids on the financial block.

Customers whose loyalty could previously be taken almost for granted were becoming increasingly sophisticated in their views of financial products and services. Also, there was new regulatory pressure on the whole financial services industry to reduce or remove the upfront and ongoing charges paid by consumers.

There were opportunities as well as challenges. New legislation was creating new product possibilities such as the tax-friendly Individual Savings Accounts (ISAs) and the low-cost Stakeholder Pensions. And emerging channels to market such as the Internet held the promise of new, cost-effective ways to reach out to a whole new generation of young and affluent customers.

But Britannic's IT systems, although efficient enough for the company 'as was', were simply too limited and inflexible to support the change and expansion envisioned by the Britannic board of directors.

And so Britannic decided to use its considerable financial strength to invest some £75 million in a complete, top-to-bottom IT and business makeover. The emphasis was on scalability, flexibility, accessibility and web-enablement. At the same time the transformation would have to be effected without disruption to day-to-day business.

Speed was of the essence. Deadlines for the permitted launch of new products (eg ISAs) were looming, and Britannic was determined to lead the market in these exciting new arenas.

For such a major programme, unique in the company's history, Britannic clearly needed external help, and the next step was to find the right IT partner. Capgemini emerged from the intensive and competitive selection process as partner of choice, for several important reasons:

- demonstrable financial services experience, supported by enthusiastic references from existing clients;

- proven expertise in major IT programmes, with the ability to integrate consulting skills with change management expertise and technical capabilities;

- a proven commitment, via its OTACE (On Time and Above Customer Expectations) methodology, to keeping its promises;

- a specific solution, with costs and planned milestones, that scored highly for credibility;

- a 'cultural fit' that would ensure effective partnership;

- ready acceptance of the principle of shared risks and rewards for the programme, with penalties for failure and rewards for success.

Solution

Joint teams from Britannic and Capgemini developed a detailed solution based on several key concepts and components. These included:

1. An Integration Hub

Capgemini's Integration Hub gave Britannic Assurance the flexibility to replace systems as required with no disruption to other systems or the rest of the business, and to add new systems, including remote ones, as necessary.

2. Modular applications software

New applications software for front- and back-office processing was also developed and bespoked in partnership with Capgemini. Its modular structure had the necessary flexibility to handle existing and virtually unlimited varieties of new financial product.

3. Customer-centric systems

Customer focus was clearly key to success, with new levels of efficiency in both sales and service, and in order to achieve that, customer-centric systems and a new, unified customer database were required.

4. Genuine partnership

All project teams were 'mixed', with client and consultant members, each with identical incentives and bonuses irrespective of employer.

5. Step by monitored step

Each project within the programme was subject to an iterative process of 'achievement/assessment', ensuring that business objectives were met at each step before proceeding to the next.

6. Knowledge transfer

To support Britannic's 'Intelligent Client' model, knowledge transfer was effected continuously to ensure that Britannic staff fully understood, and could efficiently operate, every component of the new systems without vendor dependency.

7. Parallel projects

Workflow techniques were applied to the entire programme so that critical paths could be analysed and the multiplicity of projects within the programme could be progressed in parallel, thereby significantly cutting the overall timescale.

Benefits

With the entire IT transformation completed on schedule, Britannic Assurance won immediate significant benefits:

'We have been able to add vital new products to our portfolio, including the launch, on schedule, of ISAs and Stakeholder Pensions, with total confidence in the new IT systems that support them.'

'We have added significant new channels to market, including the web and a range of business and marketing partnerships with other financial services specialists.'

'The customer-centric approach to systems design has brought important benefits, including the opportunity – which we have taken – to centralise our administration.'

'The new systems have enabled us to empower all our customer-facing staff, for example by automating our call centre and plugging our salesforce into the system with mobile computing. The result has been instant access for everyone to the customer information they need to do their jobs.'

'We now have a single, comprehensive view of every customer, despite the proliferation of products and channels, and this gives us huge opportunities for cross-selling and upselling.'

Written in co-operation with Britannic plc.

CESPA

Spain's CESPA transforms people management processes via SAP-HR backed by flexible applications management services

CESPA is a group of companies covering the whole waste cycle, offering customised services for the benefit of the community and the environment. Following a long period of consolidation via mergers, acquisitions and market liberalisation, CESPA had acquired a plethora of disparate, disconnected systems to support its people management processes. The challenge was to develop a single integrated solution with SAP-HR at the heart, with transition to the euro dictating a time-critical pressure.

With vital input from Capgemini, the results are integrated HR processes, backed by a flexible Applications Management service to secure CESPA's investment, now and in future.

Client profile

Apart from being leader in its native Spain, CESPA has a presence in Portugal, Morocco and Argentina. AGBAR, undisputed leader in Spain for waste and water services and SITA, a global waste service provider, jointly own CESPA.

The group covers the entire waste cycle by offering customised services that benefit communities and their environment. CESPA delivers waste management, street cleaning and gardening services to over 12 million people and some 9,000 industrial and commercial customers. Waste management includes sorting and recycling, composting, deriving 'green' energy and landfilling.

Business issues

CESPA had undergone immense changes to its organisation since its consolidation in the early 1970s. Mergers, acquisitions and market liberalisation had introduced a plethora of small, disparate and disconnected systems and processes. Operating in a labour-intensive industry, this was especially true for people management and HR.

It was impossible for senior management at CESPA to know exactly what constituted individual employee contracts, considerable in number, and the impact of numerous labour laws affecting them.

The situation posed high risk to CESPA – systems did not provide management with the degree of accuracy, control or quality that was a must for a people-based employer. HR represented an important part of total costs, so clearly this was an important element for CESPA to address.

Management wanted to review HR processes so that they were optimally aligned to the business. CESPA recognised that it needed a modern integrated ERP solution for HR and selected SAP-HR at the heart.

In a competitive bid tender, Capgemini demonstrated sound knowledge and experience of SAP solutions, industry know-how and innovative approaches for integration and subsequent support provision. In particular, Capgemini offered depth and breadth of services encompassing the entire spectrum from consulting excellence to flexible, innovative outsourcing services.

Solution

Capgemini deployed an experienced project team to scope the project and define a strategy to adopt. A core team comprising 10 people facilitated workshops to gather information via a template based on SAP methods.

In essence, there were four fundamental requirements, all needing to be progressed simultaneously. Apart from HR, other elements included work to get CESPA euro-ready, interfaces to financial systems, and ongoing AM (Applications Management) services. A separate team of five people developed the other projects, while a team of six commenced the core AM service.

SAP-HR was deployed across CESPA's organisation in Spain via four phases, each looking after specific geographies – Northeast centred around Barcelona, Northwest, Central and South. Due to the vast disparity of local practises and systems, a standard project rollout was impractical.

The team devised templates and checklists that maximised re-use, leveraging knowledge and experience gained to shorten subsequent phases. The first phase, lasting eight months and including a pilot, was successfully implemented in the first region.

As a result of the innovative approach, Capgemini commenced effective AM services within a month of deployment of each phase. Simultaneously, the core team moved to other regions to deploy the application, while the AM service clicked into gear. The approach facilitated ongoing AM services to commence at the earliest point in the cycle.

The next two phases lasted three months each, and the final one, representing CESPA's largest in terms of people, lasted a mere five months. Detailed project plans included agreed milestones with dates and clear responsibility for each project activity. The entire project took 19 months overall with the implementation phases lasting eight months in total.

AM services are provided remotely from Capgemini's premises near CESPA's headquarters in Barcelona. The service delivery is flexible – the number of people assigned to CESPA fluctuates as demanded by business needs.

Benefits

CESPA management is delighted with Capgemini's input. Of particular note are on-time deployment and a smooth transition to AM services before the critical target date.

The workshops facilitated by Capgemini provided CESPA with added value by getting buy-in from key stakeholders in the organisation. This built awareness of project complexities and mobilised both the business units and HR directors to support deployment.

Capgemini's experience of change management of such projects was also highly valued by CESPA management. In the live and dynamic business environment that exists at CESPA, this is an important benefit, critical for success.

Of course, the most valuable contribution to CESPA is a fully-integrated people management process and system. It allows management of the business via effective MIS. HR costs for CESPA have been transformed from a high level of uncertainty before to a high level of certainty now, with cost-reduction realised as a consequence.

The effective, flexible AM service delivered by Capgemini means that CESPA retains a sharp focus on its business in the firm knowledge that the finance and employee elements of its business have been completely transformed to serve requirements, now and in future.

'As a result of Cespa Group's growth in recent years, an integrated management of Human Resources was required. The first step was to have a system with the centralised information required to allow us to know online the current state at every moment.'

'The great challenge consisted in solving the wide diversity of contracts and dynamic character of our business, which resulted in changing requirements as we advanced.'

'We now have a base that allows us to face the future with new expectations for the development of Human Resources for our Group.'
SAP HR Manager, CESPA Group

Written in co-operation with CESPA Group.

4.3

The Coal Authority

The Coal Authority offers award-winning public service at lower cost in the UK via innovative contract yielding major benefits

The Coal Authority maintains and provides details of coal mining activity throughout Britain. Mining reports provide information on past or present coal mining operations and are a prerequisite in the conveyancing process to help solicitors, surveyors, local authorities and the general public assess the risks with a property purchase in coalfield areas.

Reporting systems were unable to support future growth in demand and were at risk of total failure. Capgemini successfully competed as partner to help design, build and run a new system to support Mining Reports, now and well into the future.

The results include far better public service at lower cost from the Authority, professionally delivered outsourcing services, and an award that prompted the IT Manager to acknowledge: 'Lots of thanks are due to our technology partners, Capgemini, who fielded a world-class team.'

Client profile

The Coal Authority, a public sector body in the UK, maintains and provides details of coal mining activity throughout Britain. The Authority supplies in excess of 500,000 mining reports a year, mainly to solicitors acting for property buyers of land on or near coalfields, past or present, in England, Scotland and Wales.

The reports give purchasers vital information about coal mining activity carried out under or near properties and are regarded by mortgage lenders, insurers etc as a fundamental prerequisite in the property purchase process.

The boom in property purchases, coupled with an explosion in re-mortgaging has led to a dramatic increase in demand for Mining Reports from the Authority.

Business issues

The Authority was determined to achieve the highest standards in the service it offered the property-buying public, and in its own cost-efficiency on behalf of the British taxpayer. However, the operational inheritance from its predecessors revolved around an outmoded 'main-frame' computer, supplemented by much use of slow, inefficient, labour-intensive pen-and-paper methods.

It was clear by the late 1990s that existing methods and IT could not fully support the faster and more responsive service that the Authority sought to provide. Systems were based on obsolete technology that was increasingly difficult to support, and, as they were not millennium compliant, were at risk of failure.

The challenge was complicated by the need to maintain and access one of the largest geographical databases in Europe. This included over 50 gigabytes of Ordnance Survey data and huge volumes of coal mining data, including paper records dating back to the 18th century. It was taking up to 10 days to respond to queries from property purchasers and solicitors. High reliance on labour-dependent processes led to potential inaccuracy. There was of course no provision for email queries. Clearly a new computer-based system, given the name MRSDS (Mining Reports and Surface Damage System), was urgently needed.

The new system would become the Authority's key IT application, lying at the heart of all its statutory activities.

Searching attention to every business requirement would therefore be vital, and in particular:

- providing rapid, accurate and comprehensive Mining Reports upon request to solicitors, surveyors, local authorities and the general public;

- improving internal efficiency and productivity in producing the reports;

- eliminating risks of systems failure that could prevent the Authority from discharging its statutory duties;

- providing safe, methodical and accessible digital storage for the Authority's collection of mining data, which forms a unique historical resource;

- catering for the needs of up to one hundred users, including staff at the Coal Authority as well as external users linking remotely;

- providing a sound and future-proof basis for direct electronic links between the Coal Authority and solicitors, other Internet users and the National Land Information Service (NLIS);

- facilitating higher volumes, in terms of systems capabilities and within contractual cost structures.

Solution

In a competitive bid, Capgemini won the contract to design, build and run MRSDS under Department of Trade and Industry PFI (Private Finance Initiative) arrangements. Capgemini would finance the initial investment, thereby absorbing the lion's share of the risk involved as well as reducing strain on the UK's public finances, and then be repaid on a long-term, per transaction basis.

The logical start was to develop a comprehensive understanding of current ways of working and a clear vision of detailed objectives of the Coal Authority. Following this, the Authority and Capgemini collaborated to develop an agreed change plan that met the ambitious new business requirements. At the heart of the plan was the need to leverage new technology so that the result was practical, reliable and cost-effective.

The next phase involved Capgemini working closely with the Authority's in-house teams to design an overall systems architecture and assess, evaluate, select and integrate several technology components within the architecture. These included:

- a Geographical Information System (GIS) to turn the huge volumes of data (over 50 gigabytes of Ordnance Survey Landline data and around two million items of primary coal mining data) into an efficient format;

- a Relational Database to enable the GIS to be searched with high speed and efficiency, and permit users to apply a variety of search criteria;

- a Workflow System to ensure rapid turnaround of enquiries, with automatic compliance checks at every stage and prompts to ensure adherence to timetable on each individual piece of work;

- the Workflow system had to include a new facility to record and cost every enquiry;

- a Windows user-friendly front-end to replace the specialised, non-intuitive and unappealing monochrome screens previously used.

The MRSDS system was based on an adaptive architecture, and Capgemini leveraged its strategic alliances with partners such as IBM, Oracle, SUN and HP to ensure a solution that matched requirements.

The project used PRINCE – **PR**ojects **IN** Controlled **E**nvironments – as the methodology, and was jointly managed and staffed by the Authority and Capgemini. Extensive two-way knowledge transfer was a permanent feature. The jointly staffed project organisation, steered by a Project Board, included three teams looking after specific phases – Design Analysis and Data Migration, Change Management, and Quality Assurance.

At the same time, plans were enacted for Capgemini to deliver services for Infrastructure Management (IM) on the entire infrastructure supporting the Authority and Applications Management (AM) on MRSDS.

Leveraging a centre-based, remote delivery approach, services for IM commenced from Capgemini's Centre of Excellence in Rotherham. Upon successful deployment of MRSDS, Capgemini commenced AM services on the application from its AMSC (Applications Management Service Centre) in Bristol.

Benefits

The new MRSDS system and its ongoing management on an outsourcing basis have met each and every objective set by the Coal Authority, providing a rare example of outstanding success in a PFI contract. Specifically:

- turnaround times have been reduced from 10 to two days in most cases, with a 24-hour service for email queries, fully in line with the objectives of the Coal Authority at inception;

- costs have been significantly cut as a result of the improved efficiency of the new system, leading to a big reduction in wasteful clerical and manual effort. It has also helped the Authority to rationalise two sites into one, with further significant savings in location;

- staff can be brought up to speed in a much shorter time. The integrated workflow, administration and GIS databases have removed the need for complex business process training; in effect, the expertise is designed into the system;

- the savings have been passed on to customers, reducing the cost of a standard Mining Report by 25 per cent;

- customer satisfaction (formally measured at least annually) has risen to record levels, with 86.5 per cent rating the Authority's performance as 'excellent' or 'good' in key areas and less than 0.5 per cent rating it as unsatisfactory. Some 71.5 per cent rate the Authority as better than other information providers in the conveyancing process;

- the project has demonstrated the commitment of the Coal Authority to customers and a determination to introduce modern techniques supported by investment in new technology;

- the risk of systems failure has been greatly reduced by Capgemini's failsafe procedures;

- information that previously existed in a variety of paper and online systems, incapable of being effectively interrogated or analysed for its impact on any given single location, is now dynamically available via a single enquiry;

- the complex technical environment and innovative requirements made it inevitable that obstacles would arise, but the excellent partnership forged from the start by the Coal Authority and Capgemini proved invaluable in overcoming these obstacles and was a key factor in the very successful implementation;

- the new system has handled a 90 per cent expansion in volumes with less than pro-rata staff increases;

- a major improvement in an important public service has been effected without imposing any unnecessary burden on public spending.

Senior managers at the Coal Authority, delighted with results so far, have agreed to a new contract with Capgemini.

The project success led to the Coal Authority receiving the annual BCS IS Management Award. Here are some comments from senior Coal Authority officers at the awards ceremony:

'It was previously a 'paperchase' system. This project has allowed us to combine all processes into one to give us a fast, accurate, cost-effective, high-volume service.'

'We now make better use of staff. With the previous system we had highly-qualified technical staff doing the work. We now have staff more tied to things we need to do, and the ratio of non-technical to technical staff in this area is now 4:1.'
Mining Reports Manager

'When we started we had mainframe systems, Cobol and Fortran systems. With the millennium issues about to come up, the Coal Authority didn't have the money to do the build or know-how to manage all the risks involved, so we put together the public finance initiative approach and used Capgemini, who understood the risks and the maturity of the business.'

'It is an incredible privilege to win this award, and it would not have been possible without the co-operation of quite an extensive team.'
IT Manager

Written in co-operation with the Coal Authority.

4.4

Corus

Outsourced IT proves crucial to success of global business transformation – 'The Corus advantage is IT'

Corus, one of the world's leading manufacturers, processors and distributors of steel and steel-based solutions, was formed just ahead of the new millennium by the merger of British Steel and Koninklijke Hoogovens. A key challenge was to achieve a unified approach to marketing opportunities and production needs based on two entirely separate IT heritages.

Capgemini was already in place in the UK arm of Corus, running virtually the entire UK IT operation in a long-term outsourcing contract signed before the merger. It was asked to work in partnership with Corus senior management and other service providers in a further 'great leap forward' in IT to help Corus achieve its new vision.

The result is ongoing IT support with no disruption or loss of continuity with service levels maintained at 99 per cent plus of the time. Some 20 per cent savings in the considerable IT annual budget for Corus have been realised.

Client profile

Corus is one of the world's leading manufacturers, processors and distributors of steel and steel-based solutions. Formed just ahead of the new millennium by the merger of British Steel plc and Koninklijke Hoogovens NV, Corus is a customer-focused, innovative, solutions-driven company, which combines international expertise with local service.

Corus has 20 Business Units world-wide, delivering innovative solutions to a broad range of markets, including construction, automotive, packaging, aerospace, energy and engineering industries.

The company's strategy aims to create shareholder value by achieving world-class competitiveness through operating excellence and technological advance. The emphasis of Corus investments is in down-stream added-value activities, which can achieve leading positions in attractive market sectors with sustainable growth.

Business issues

Global over-capacity, government-subsidised competition and protectionist barriers to free trade have all helped to make today's international steel industry one of the toughest businesses of all time.

The successful fight-back by Corus against these challenges has been based on two strategic concepts:

- the ongoing re-invention of the company as a provider of steel-based solutions as opposed to a producer of bulk tonnage of steel, with a new emphasis on innovation and close partnership with customers;

- the pursuit – and achievement – of world-class standards in manufacturing and distribution, with new efficiencies facilitated by automation, streamlined operations and robotics, and with all processes throughout the business supported by world-class IT.

A key challenge for Corus was how to achieve a unified approach to its marketing opportunities and its production needs based on two entirely separate IT heritages: those of the two merging companies. The problem was compounded by the fact that both British Steel and Koninklijke

Hoogovens had themselves grown largely by acquisition, resulting in a diversity of IT systems which, although having rich functionality and great fitness for purpose, were not interfacing with one another as Corus management's new vision required.

An additional challenge for Corus was to make appropriate use of the new web-based technologies, both in its internal communications and knowledge management and its external procurement and sales activities.

Solution

Capgemini was already in place in the UK arm of Corus, running virtually the entire IT operation (hardware, software and networking at Corporate, Business Unit and Plant levels) in a long-term outsourcing contract signed in 1997 with the former British Steel. Performance on this contract was manifestly on target, with significant improvements in IT service, reductions in IT costs and, most crucial of all, major contributions to the steel company's overall competitiveness. Capgemini was therefore asked to work in partnership with Corus senior management in a further 'great leap forward' in IT that would help the company achieve its new vision.

The programme undertaken by Capgemini and Corus was built on three main foundations:

1. Integration

The new streamlined, integrated, energy-efficient manufacturing processes being introduced by Corus demanded equally integrated IT. Yet the special needs of steel manufacture, and the fact that the systems in place were custom-designed to meet those needs, ruled out their wholesale replacement by a new, off-the-peg ERP solution. The 'hourglass' shape of the Corus business involved multiple raw material inputs being brought together into a vast range of outputs – tubes, pipes, coils, sheets, pressings etc. Moreover, their properties then needed to be traced in further processing at Corus and beyond. All this was simply beyond the capabilities of any standardised applications packages on the market.

The solution determined was therefore to aim for greatly enhanced integration of existing applications. Preserving data integrity and achieving seamless communication between a large number of disparate applications called for systems integration skills of a high order, and these Capgemini was able to supply. The approach taken also effectively lengthened the useful life of hardware and applications software already in place, and therefore increased the ROI on the existing investment in IT, while eliminating the need for a massive investment in totally new systems.

2. Standardisation

It was clear that one key factor determining the success of the merger that created Corus would be the ability to function as a single, fully-connected company, able to communicate effectively from site to site and country to country. Capgemini and Corus therefore put a high priority on a phased programme of standardisation. Areas such as desktop facilities and communications, knowledge communities and databases, web access and protocols were all included in the programme, with a strong focus on establishing agreed common standards and putting in place procedures to ensure compliance to those standards.

3. Flexibility

The new focus on Corus as a customer-driven solutions company, launching many new products every year, highlighted the need for flexibility of IT support. To succeed in fast-moving market sectors, Corus would need the capability to move equally fast, and therefore the idea of hard-wiring systems 'forever' was rapidly reaching its sell-by-date. Capgemini was therefore tasked with giving Corus' UK systems a degree of flexibility never envisaged when they were originally installed. The power and resources of the world-wide web would be key to this new flexibility. Capgemini worked with Corus in both a consulting and implementation capacity to establish a new, secure, user-friendly Corus portal. The portal would permit customers, suppliers, partners and employees to obtain the information they needed without risk to the integrity of the core Corus systems now being connected to the web.

Benefits

The Chief Information Officer at Corus outlined the benefits achieved midway through the Capgemini 10-year contract as follows:

'Corus is undergoing a successful global transformation from a supplier of bulk steel tonnage to a provider of customer-driven solutions, and that change could not have taken place without the progress we have made in IT assisted by outsourcing support to a world-class IT partner.'

'Significant progress has been made in integrating our IT to support a new and more streamlined way of running our business. This equates to significant benefits in terms of manufacturing costs, supply chain effectiveness and customer service – both in terms of delivering the right quality products with great alacrity and in terms of having up-to-the-minute information for the customer on progress against contract.'

'We have seen some highly significant quick wins from our standardisation programme with, for example, the thousands of desktops in our business able to communicate with common email tools from Day One of the merger. Standardisation of our Lotus Notes facility is providing a new level of support for our knowledge communities and enabling us to function more effectively as a unified business.'

'Underlying all the challenging new projects that it has delivered to time and budget, Capgemini has also maintained our ongoing day-to-day IT support with no disruption or loss of continuity. I expect service levels to be maintained 99 per cent plus of the time and Capgemini meets this expectation.'

'The objective of driving down IT costs (while radically improving our IT) was key to the original plan to outsource, and performance against plan has exceeded our expectations, with some 20 per cent savings in our very considerable IT annual budget being realised to date. Perhaps equally important, by outsourcing to a provider like Capgemini, using 'open book' methods, we now know and fully understand our IT costs, and how benefits and costs are related.'

'Significantly improved IT has enabled many parts of our business to achieve reduced stockholdings despite increased throughput, with significant progress towards the "just-in-time" approach that has revolutionised many sectors of manufacturing.'

'Capgemini has been instrumental in helping us integrate our existing systems with the world-wide web, and helping us reap the benefits of e-commerce as buyers, sellers and partners. This has also facilitated a new style of co-operative working with many of our major customers, sharing knowledge with them via the web on major development projects.'

'By using their systems integration and middleware expertise, Capgemini has extended the life of our existing investment in IT, and therefore improved the effective return on investment, and has also given them the modern look and feel of web-based systems, with resulting improvements in user-friendliness.'

'Capgemini has taken the time and trouble to understand our large and complex business, and to explain IT, and what information technology can do, to our managers at all levels in demystified, acronym-free terms, and although not quantifiable, this is a benefit of tremendous importance to Corus.'

The CIO for Corus summarises the progress made by saying:

'Today we can state with confidence that in supporting our new business vision and in delivering competitive advantage, the Corus advantage is IT.'

Written in co-operation with Corus plc.

DARA

DARA on fast track toward adaptive enterprise for UK defence aviation repairs business

DARA (Defence Aviation Repair Agency) is a business in the middle of unprecedented change, within an industry that has itself seen extraordinary volatility in recent years.

DARA had to move from being a government agency to a fully competitive commercial organisation, and sought partnership with Capgemini via a £33 million engagement.

Major performance gains are already a reality. These include reduction in the time taken to undertake full maintenance of a VC10 tanker aircraft from 180 days to 95 days, and servicing Sea King helicopter engines from 185 to 57 days.

Client profile

Once part of the MoD (Ministry of Defence) in the UK, DARA is on a direct route to becoming a totally independent business, already trading commercially on the open market. DARA was the result of an amalgamation of two separate agencies – Royal Air Force and Royal Navy.

Between them, the agencies shared responsibility for servicing and maintenance of all aircraft owned by the British defence establishment. This included several hundred fast jets, a substantial fleet of helicopters and large jets used for passenger transport and in-flight refuelling.

Given the strategic nature of the business, the two agencies had always focused on exceptional levels of quality performance but had not always matched technical excellence with equivalent commercial thinking.

Business issues

As part of a new approach to some aspects of defence management in the UK, the aim was for DARA to become an independent company. Although it was to continue working on MoD contracts, it also needed to take on work in the commercial sector for other clients at home and abroad. The first step was for DARA to become a 'trading fund' within the MoD, with operations and commercial results separated from the Ministry.

The importance of a move towards full spares-inclusive trading, an ambitious goal for such a major development, cannot be overstated. It involved new thinking, attitudes and strategies and demanded a clear-sighted evaluation of DARA's own systems and operations.

These were fundamental requisites in order to achieve the levels of efficiency needed to compete in the open market. That market had seen extraordinary pressures in recent years – demand fluctuation and competition balanced by an incessant drive for cost reduction. For DARA, the required transformation brought major challenges.

DARA had to move from having a single, albeit, important customer to seeking business all over Europe, and from being purely a defence business to servicing commercial companies. This had to be against a backdrop of an industry with intense competition – contractual relationships were rapidly evolving into new forms.

Scalability was essential to cope with rapid variation in demand – clients were moving towards service contracts with payment linked to results. Flexibility, speed and high efficiency were critical success factors. The DARA vision was to deliver:

- a world-class aircraft maintenance facility providing outstanding 'Turn Time' performance and quality at a competitive price;
- specialised service/product approaches;
- customer focus;
- high levels of skills and innovation to meet customer expectations.

Managing such change required a revolution in culture, attitudes and skills. There was also another major challenge to overcome: a concurrent transformation of current processes and systems. DARA had inherited an infrastructure that reflected the past, not the future. It had four widely scattered sites, chosen for their proximity to major defence establishments rather than on commercial logic.

At the same time, haphazard investment over several years had left DARA with a legacy of 52 separate systems. Clear, decisive action was necessary so that DARA was ready to compete in the commercial world.

DARA had already made the decision to make processes the first priority. No radical change in performance was possible until the tangle of different systems were replaced by a single, integrated set of enterprise processes, optimised for speed, efficiency and scaleable working. DARA invested in Baan's aerospace ERP system, and asked Capgemini to lead the implementation across the business.

Capgemini was selected for proven capabilities to deliver complex change projects involving multiple dimensions of people, processes and technology. It also demonstrated deep expertise of the MRO (Maintenance Repair and Overhaul) toolset deployed in the supply chain industry.

Solution

Capgemini proposed to re-engineer DARA business processes to incorporate a full redesign of commercial planning, production, materials management, finance, new service provision and data management. The redesign would facilitate a full programme of change management, supported by the Baan system.

A single, seamlessly integrated team, with Capgemini, Baan and DARA personnel came together in a highly efficient way. The team removed all artificial boundaries between them to scope the project, develop strategies and deploy solutions, and adopted a composite methodology to drive results. The methodology comprised best practice from industry-specific approaches, Baan's own method and Capgemini's quality system, DELIVER. Several elements of the collaboration included:

Skills transfer

It was recognised quite early on that skills and experience were critical aspects, and there was strong emphasis on skills transfer, with DARA people being given unqualified support to develop their own expertise to new levels as the project continued.

Customer focus

The work remained highly customer-focused, with emphasis on the kind of results most valued by commercial clients. That included giving the team visibility across the full supply chain, backed by a capability to develop holistic solutions for customers.

Transformational outsourcing

The long-term management of specialised systems was turned into a flexible outsourcing contract, again managed by Capgemini. The nature of the outsourcing service addresses DARA's requirement for maximum scalability and efficiency in an evolving manner.

Project implementation is ongoing, stage by stage. Experience and skills from Capgemini's broad portfolio of services is leveraged to drive results at each step of the way. These range from Strategy Consulting, Supply Chain, Technology Consulting and Outsourcing.

The new system is already live at the smallest of DARA's four major sites, and plans to deploy to remaining sites over the next few months are well advanced. Legacy systems will be decommissioned as soon as the new system has been deployed in all sites.

Following completion of the core ERP deployment, the transformational element of the outsourcing service will come into play when the programme encompasses DARA's 'outer circle'. This includes connecting the ERP system to core external industry systems as well as to DECS.

The latter is one of the most sophisticated online marketplaces in the world, jointly developed by the MoD and Capgemini.

Management at DARA clearly demonstrate satisfaction with Capgemini's input to date and have awarded a 3-year outsourcing contract valued at over £30 million. This covers IM (Infrastructure Management) for the entire IT infrastructure at DARA, together with AM (Applications Management) services, including the Baan system.

Services for IM are delivered from Capgemini's secure data centre at Toltec, near Bristol. This includes a help-desk for some 5,000 staff at all DARA sites in England, Wales and Scotland. AM services are delivered remotely from Capgemini's Applications Management Service Centre in Sale, Cheshire.

Benefits

Not only will implementation of the Baan ERP approach at DARA provide greater responsiveness and flexibility in action; it will enable better management of all processes in one comprehensive system. That includes assessing the value of contracts, improving financial controls and ensuring close integration of production, scheduling and supply chain.

Driving the process of rapid implementation and development are facts of life that DARA now deals with:

- the need for responsiveness, being able to cope at high speed with the need to expand or contract to fit fluctuating market demands;

- the need to deliver a set of customised solutions that precisely fit the non-standard requirements of very different customers;

- the need to have a transparent, highly efficient but very secure supply chain based on flexible relationships and, potentially, facilitated by digital exchanges;

- above all, the need to manage costs in a business where lack of accurate information at the right moment can wipe out the profit on a major piece of business.

The work carried out at DARA is ultimately about assuring the very future of the company.

One key benefit of the outsourcing service from Capgemini to DARA is to provide economies of scale. Service delivery adopts an 'industrialised' concept of shared resources and manpower to many clients, meaning that DARA pays for a service, not a fixed number of resources. These elements facilitate transformational outsourcing for DARA's benefit.

Most important of all, the entire DARA organisation is now more flexible and ready for change. The success of the changes undertaken so far has helped to breed more adaptive attitudes throughout the company. This, together with the inherently greater fluidity of the new processes now in place, makes DARA able to face the future in this highly unpredictable market with confidence.

In the words of the Chief Executive for DARA:

'As a commercial enterprise operating in highly competitive international defence markets, we must ensure that customers and customer service are our prime focus, and that our information systems support every part of our business in meeting that objective.'

'Capgemini has clearly demonstrated the commitment and capability to deliver the world-class IT service that we, as a customer-facing organisation, know to be vital.'

Commenting on the outsourcing elements of the partnership, the CEO adds:

'Outsourcing our IT to world-class professionals will also boost our ability to respond rapidly to whatever new needs may emerge in the fast-changing worlds of aviation and defence.'

Written in co-operation with DARA.

GM Europe

Pan-European e-business websites link General Motors across languages, cultures and business processes

General Motors (GM), the world's largest vehicle manufacturer, designs, builds and markets cars and trucks world wide. GM was determined to lead the industry in all aspects of e-business. The aim was to develop and deploy practical, user-friendly websites that would deliver real service to the consumer and add real value to the business.

GM had already developed the essential technology known as GlobalBuy Power (GBP). Its next challenge was implementation and deployment: how to make this new IT actually work across 12 different European countries each with its own language, culture, business partners and the GM organisation. Capgemini deployed websites linked to IT systems in 'real time' to production, distribution and financing as well as third-party systems (eg dealers' websites).

As a result of savings, deployment costs were reduced by 53 per cent below budget. The project enabled GM to avoid the high costs of individual initiatives in each country. It has also reduced ongoing web-hosting costs and delivered rapid results. The project became one of only three 'projects of the year' throughout GM to win an internal award for meaning most to eGM in terms of learning, impact, and establishing General Motors as an e-corporation.

Client profile

General Motors (GM), the world's largest vehicle manufacturer, designs, builds and markets cars and trucks worldwide. In a recent year, GM earned $1.5 billion on sales of $177.3 billion, excluding special items. It employs about 362,000 people globally.

GM has been the world's automotive sales leader since 1931. Founded in 1908, GM today has manufacturing operations in more than 30 countries and its vehicles are sold in about 200 countries. In 2001, GM sold more than 8.5 million cars and trucks – more than any other auto-maker and 15.1 per cent of the world vehicle market. GM's major markets are North America, Europe, Asia-Pacific, Latin America, Africa and the Middle East.

GM cars and trucks are sold under the following brands: Chevrolet, Pontiac, Buick, Oldsmobile, Cadillac, GMC, Saturn, Hummer, Saab, Opel, Vauxhall and Holden. GM parts and accessories are marketed under the GM, GM Goodwrench and ACDelco brands through GM Service Parts Operations.

Business issues

As the world's largest car-maker, GM was determined to lead the industry in all aspects of e-business and not least in its dealings with customers, actual and potential. The aim was to develop and deploy practical, user-friendly websites that would deliver real service to the consumer and add real value to the business – and to do so rapidly, without glitches, ahead of its competitors and in partnership with its dealers.

Users would be able, from their homes or offices, to review the GM range and select a vehicle matching their lifestyle requirements, configure and cost it, book a testdrive, review finance schemes and costs, review warranty details and arrange credit.

GM had already developed the essential technology in the form of a suite of advanced systems known as GBP. Its next challenge was implementation and deployment: how to make this new IT actually work across 12 different European countries (Croatia, Czech Republic, Denmark, Finland, Hungary, Ireland, Norway, Poland, Portugal, Slovak Republic, Slovenia and Spain), each with its own language, culture, business partners and GM organisation.

Websites were, from the start, conceived to go far beyond the static, 'electronic brochure' pattern. Rather, they would be 'live', fully interactive, and kept constantly updated.

The IT systems supporting them would therefore need to link in 'real time' with a whole spectrum of existing GM IT systems (eg on production, distribution and financing information), as well as third-party IT systems (eg dealers' websites).

Solution

GM Europe knew that external help would be vital to get its ambitious programme completed rapidly. The original plan was to use an existing partner for deployment, but there was concern about the cost-efficiency of the rollout approach.

Following a review of alternative deployment partners, GM Europe chose Capgemini, and for three major reasons:

- credible and cost-effective proposals;

- proven expertise in systems integration and in the management of major IT programmes;

- excellent track record in working in close and effective partnership with GM.

Initially selected for the GBP rollout in Norway, Capgemini not only successfully completed the assignment in a 'timetable-busting' four months, but – equally important – demonstrated how GM could halve its deployment costs and, through re-use of Norwegian delivery processes, reduce them still further. As a result, Capgemini was awarded the deployment contract for the remaining European countries.

Capgemini organised the project into three major workstreams:

1. Project management and control

This workstream including such areas as:

- refinement and rigorous application of an existing and proven deployment methodology;
- management and control of third-party vendors;
- reporting and communications across all project streams;
- capture, management and re-use of knowledge.

2. Information systems

IT tools and techniques deployed by the joint GM Europe/Capgemini team included:

- formalised, consistent deployment methods used across all 12 countries to enhance speed, reduce costs and avoid duplication of effort;
- visual (chart-based) high-level centralised planning and progress tools to support parallel deployment in several countries at once
- formal risk/issue/change management processes from the outset.

3. Business processes

These included:

- metrics and benefit tracking to measure the business impact of GBP;
- strategy communication within GM and the dealer community;
- business resource impact of GBP.

The Capgemini streaming principle was a key enabler in ensuring that work on all fronts could go ahead rapidly and simultaneously, and with full co-ordination between the various subteams.

A key factor in each of the 12 individual country deployment projects was the application of Capgemini's OTACE ('On Time and Above Customer Expectations') methodology. It is a management tool, used at the start of every project to establish the factors considered by the client to be crucial to success, together with agreed metrics for evaluating performance against those factors. It goes all the way up to the 'CEO perspective' to give the 'big picture' of how well Capgemini performed and just what contribution the project has made, once completed, to the success of the client's business. And it goes all the way down to 'supervisor' level to look at each individual project objective in the finest numerical detail. OTACE is mandatory on all Capgemini projects of significant size. In the case of the GBP projects at GM Europe, all 12 achieved outstandingly high OTACE scores, and the OTACE discipline was itself highly commended by GM senior management.

Meeting the challenges

The multi-country GBP project presented a number of unusual challenges:

- What appears to the casual observer to be a simple website is actually a complex, web-based application. It requires a mass of vehicle option and dealer data from a number of existing GM corporate data systems. In addition, it is integrated with GM's finance and dealer website pages in each country.

- At the start of Capgemini's involvement, GM already had a deployment partner, but deliberately decided not to ask Capgemini to adopt their existing partner's established practice. Instead, Capgemini was asked to start with a 'clean sheet of paper' and propose a fresh approach.

- The Global GM project worked around the US working day, and deployment partners accommodated themselves to these hours, wherever they may be in the world.

- Capgemini ensured that third parties from many companies and countries delivered, to the team's project plans.

- There were many specific business deployment drivers that had to be achieved (eg motor shows promoting the site).

A true partnership

From day one, Capgemini and GM Europe established a multinational 'virtual team', with every member able to call on the expertise and experience of both companies. A strong commitment to formal communications (eg through regular team briefings, progress reports and a special project website) was supplemented by a wide range of jointly sponsored social activities.

Benefits

The deployment of GBP was completed in all 12 countries successfully and ahead of the very tightly-planned timescale in every case. In many countries the projects were completed far ahead of schedule to fit in with the timing of national motor shows.

As a result of savings made possible by Capgemini techniques, deployment costs were reduced by 53 per cent below budget. The project enabled GM to avoid the high costs of individual initiatives in each country. It has also reduced ongoing web-hosting costs and delivered rapid results and website consistency across all 12 countries.

Consequently, GM has become the first major motor company to have in place a consistent, full-function internet offering for consumers across Europe. The GBP project underwent an internal 'Project Health Check' by GM's Information Systems & Services quality organisation. It received a 100 per cent quality rating. The project also became one of only three 'projects of the year' throughout GM to win an internal award for the projects, that meant most to eGM in terms of learning, impact, and establishing General Motors as an e-corporation. By the conclusion of the whole 12-country project, Capgemini had received many messages of thanks and appreciation from GM executives across Europe.

To sum up the whole project, we end by quoting (with the kind permission of the author) the whole text of a letter sent by GM Europe's Deployment Manager for GBP to the Capgemini Account Director:

'As we near the close of our current GM Europe project, I am writing to express my sincere appreciation for the exceptional efforts put forth by your team. With our final countries going "live" in September, we will be on our way to exceeding our goals with over 18 countries deployed on GM Global BuyPower across Europe. We have been able to achieve a reduction in costs to deploy over 53 per cent while increasing our ration of countries deployed by 3.5 times.

'Deploying a global application can be challenging and difficult. It is very hard to work in different time zones in different countries with varied cultures and perspectives. Adding operational "growing pains", management teams on multiple continents, and changing requirement, made this a daunting endeavour. Despite this, and as a direct result of your team's efforts, GM Europe has taken a leadership position in deployment at eGM and is looked to as the example of "how to do it right"!

'Credibility is everything and your team has loads. Without diminishing the efforts of everyone, I especially want to highlight the efforts of certain individuals. I truly believe their contributions have made the difference between a complete and a highly successful project. Dedication, attention to details, and willingness to do what's right has made this project a memorable experience for me.'

Written in co-operation with General Motors.

4.7

Hydro One

Hydro One in Canada outsources technology services and business process management to Capgemini

Full market liberalisation of the Canadian energy sector was fast approaching. Hydro One Networks Inc., as owner and operator of one of the largest transmission and distribution systems in North America, needed to be ready.

Confident that it offered an effective strategy, Capgemini was selected by Hydro One as its business and IT outsourcing partner.

The result is a ground-breaking, billion-dollar transformational outsourcing contract that sees Capgemini delivering comprehensive technology-enabled and business process management services to Hydro One over 10 years.

Client profile

Hydro One Networks Inc., a subsidiary of Hydro One Inc., owns and operates the largest electricity transmission and distribution system in Ontario, serving about 1.2 million customers.

Hydro One operates a high-voltage electricity transmission system and a largely rural low-voltage distribution system throughout the province. It represents one of the 10 largest electricity transmission and distribution systems in North America.

The passage of the Electricity Act in 1998 fundamentally restructured Ontario's electricity industry. By the following April, transmission and distribution wire operations became regulated by the Ontario Energy Board (OEB) by law. The industry started the transition towards competitive bidding in the wholesale and retail electricity markets, with the energy market scheduled to open competition within three years.

Responsible for the former Ontario Hydro transmission and distribution wires facilities, the mandate for Hydro One Networks Inc. was to:

- operate, maintain and administer its transmission and distribution facilities in a safe and reliable manner;

- continuously improve operating efficiencies;

- facilitate access to the electricity supply marketplace in Ontario.

Business issues

In order to be successful under the new market conditions, Hydro One had to streamline its business. It had to be leaner and more cost-effective. To be prepared for a competitive environment, management chose to focus on building Hydro One's core wires business. Non-core, yet essential functions were taking up valuable time and resources and Hydro One's management understood that these functions could be more efficiently managed by an experienced third party.

The sheer scale of deregulation activity in the sector globally was presenting alternative and proven approaches to managing non-core components of the utility business. Examples from around the world, and in Ontario, provided Hydro One with successful examples of solutions and best practices adopted by players facing similar challenges.

Management at Hydro One had been following one particular example very closely. The approach, in that instance, included a unique, innovative solution, one that had been watched with much interest throughout the global energy and utility community. The solution, having found root some 18 months earlier had Capgemini as the partner, delivering IT services through existing infrastructure and technology. Capgemini had been providing consulting services to Hydro One for a number of years. This long-standing relationship provided evidence of Capgemini's leadership role in the Canadian energy and utility industry and gave Hydro One confidence in its partner's ability to deliver results on time and within budget.

Following a competitive bid tender, Hydro One awarded a landmark $1 billion CDN contract to Capgemini to manage and operate technology-enabled services to Hydro One over 10 years.

'This arrangement with Capgemini will allow Hydro One to achieve cost saving and now focus on providing safe and reliable delivery of electricity at competitive prices.'

Solution

A number of elements differentiated Capgemini's proposal, including:

- experience with local labour groups;
- service delivery from the Toronto area to facilitate workforce reduction by Hydro One without loss of the skills;
- aggressive pricing based on knowledge of business;
- leverage pre-existing IT infrastructure and resources;
- leverage relationship with Vertex for CRM-based solutions.

These elements, when combined with Capgemini's capabilities across people, process, technology and knowledge management, facilitated the development of effective solutions, executed in close collaboration with Hydro One.

The strategy was underpinned by one fundamental principle – lower costs through economies of scale. This was going to be achieved by leveraging specialised services being delivered by Capgemini to other clients from a dedicated service delivery centre in Toronto. Capgemini's delivery centre manages and delivers technology-enabled and business process management services.

In the transition process, about 900 employees transferred their employment from Hydro One to Capgemini. The due diligence process was successfully completed, according to the contract and on time.

Capgemini then commenced delivery of HR, finance and settlements, supply chain management services, IT and infrastructure support to Hydro One, with Vertex, a valued partner, providing customer care support to the utility. The delivery centre offers unique and specialised outsourcing services to major Canadian utilities and other industry sectors. Combined, over 1,500 full-time and contract employees provide expertise to support enterprise technology, business process and IT management services.

These services are not just provided to Hydro One, but also to Ontario Power Generation, Nuclear Safety Solutions and Bruce Power. The dedicated centre has the capability and infrastructure to provide back-office and IT support to utilities and other companies across North America. It is this element of the approach that takes the capabilities of Capgemini beyond traditional outsourcing.

Benefits

Management at Hydro One is pleased with the consistent delivery of services during the first year of the contract, when significant changes in the Ontario electricity marketplace were taking place. Developed in collaboration, with close attention paid to detail, the service illustrates effective partnership with Capgemini. The professionally delivered service is comprehensive, encompassing:

Information technology

This includes enterprise technology services, infrastructure management, network outsourcing, applications management and support.

Business process management

This covers finance and accounting, payroll, settlements (wholesale, retail, data management) customer care (contact centre, billing, collections), supply management services (demand management, strategic sourcing, logistics).

As a result, Hydro One can:

- focus on its core wires business, with the flexibility to adapt to change as required;

- develop a competitive pricing structure based on cost savings;

- enjoy cost savings from economies of scale.

In an effort to improve customer service, enhance operational efficiencies and continue to reduce costs, Capgemini implemented a speech recognition solution as part of the customer care component of the contract. Speech recognition software has the ability to recognise general, naturally flowing utterances from a wide variety of users. It recognises the caller's answers to move along the flow of the call.

Hydro One's customers have been enjoying the convenience of obtaining account information, entering their meter reading or reporting a power outage using the speech recognition system. As a consequence, the daily percentage of calls successfully completed using the software has increased between five and 10 per cent.

Another benefit of the arrangement is to the 900 employees who were transferred to Capgemini. They comprise the core of Capgemini's delivery centre and are able to leverage their experience to serve their former employer, now a valued customer.

As a result of this arrangement, Hydro One management retains focus on its core wires business in the knowledge that essential functions of its non-core business are in capable hands.

Written in co-operation with Hydro One Inc.

Mercedes-Benz USA

Widening the Mercedes-Benz window of confidence: comfort, style, performance, security and applications management services

'In a perfect world everyone would drive a Mercedes.' Thanks to a long-term relationship and a strong delivery team, Mercedes-Benz USA LLC (MBUSA) management was convinced that Capgemini was well positioned, due to its Applications Management and Infrastucture Management track record, to provide staff and maintenance services for the Claim Analysis and Reimbursement System (MBCAReS).

The objectives of MBUSA were to support integrated world-wide production, accommodate a single European market, satisfy changing client expectations, optimise costs, replace outdated technology and introduce new warranty processing methods.

Client profile

Known for superbly-engineered luxury and prestige in automotives, MBUSA manufactures, sells and services passenger cars and trucks as a private subsidiary of Daimler-Benz Corporation North America. MBUSA's headquarters for Mercedes-Benz USA is Montvale, NJ.

Mercedes-Benz Retail Centres pride themselves on providing top-quality, competitively priced services and associated parts. The company reputation is built on craftsmanship, performance, safety and value. Mercedes-Benz vehicles are designed using the most advanced technology, as company marketing says, 'We know every last nut and bolt intimately, which is why we can offer the best replacement parts for your vehicle'.

Business issues

Usual procedures for Mercedes owners with a car under warranty that needed repairs meant the owner would arrange for repair at a local Mercedes Service Center and it was the service centre that assumed the repair costs.

But following the DaimlerChrysler merger, new corporate rules established at European DaimlerChrylser AG (DCAG) headquarters determined warranty reimbursement standards to dealers in the USA and Canada. MBUSA was now asked to pass authorisation for warranty claim repairs through DCAG in Europe for warranty reimbursement. This was a very complex, time-consuming process, to recoup the warranty payments after the US dealers had already serviced the cars. MBUSA already had an MBCAReS in place before the DaimlerChrysler merger.

The new rule-based system of warranty claims processing parameters needed to be adaptable to each country and individual market. In the past, warranty claim processing was mainly a manual task, relying on two different IT systems (MBUSA Warranty system and the DCAG system).

Keeping an eye on efficiency and cost control, the need was to modify the German DCAG IT system to meet market requirements. Mercedes-Benz would benefit immensely from one common claims processing system.

To globally standardise the organisation, to eliminate complexity and to reduce costs of supporting two IT systems Daimler-Benz required all its world-wide subsidiaries to migrate to an IBM platform. Objectives were to:

• support integrated world-wide production;

• satisfy changing client expectations;

• optimise associated costs;

• replace antiquated technologies;

• introduce new warranty processing philosophies.

In order to achieve this, MBUSA was looking for supplemental support and assistance to meet time commitments integrating multiple platforms.

As a result of a long-term relationship with MBUSA and a consistently successful delivery track record, Capgemini was asked to provide Applications Management on MBCAReS.

MBUSA was already using IBM as their mainframe vendor; however, their Integrated Vehicle Preparation Centre Inventory System supporting remote facilities was using a DEC VAX/VMS platform. The need was to interface the parts ordering systems in order to allow access to a second platform by replacing the DEC system with the same functionality and consolidate with IBM mainframes. This would position MBUSA with a world-wide system having global capabilities.

Solution

MBUSA partnered with Capgemini on MBCAReS. MBUSA was the pilot location for this project, which has since been introduced into other countries. MBCAReS was jointly developed by both the business units and IT divisions of Mercedes-Benz. Capgemini provide supplemental support staff, maintenance and applications management services for the MBCAReS system: a Project Management Office (PMO) and JAVA development engagement on project Netstar.

Although the project development was shared with Germany, strict guidelines co-ordinated documentation, language and cultural differences. Project logistics overcame geographical distance, different time windows, languages, and travel, which proved significantly challenging as a project on a critical timeline.

Capgemini presented several possible platform scenarios, and MBUSA chose IBM RISC 6000, running Micro Focus COBOL under the AIX operating system as the new IVIS platform. MBCAReS is now in the 'support mode'. MBUSA components were turned over to DCAG for introduction into other countries, assuring:

- User support – managing user requests for application-related assistance; requests for information; problem logging; problem tracking; trend analysis;

- Maintenance – production support (24x7x365) including on-call support (after business hours) corrective and preventive maintenance;

- Enhancements (650 hours per month) – including modification of existing software, the development of new software or the installation of software packages to respond to regulatory, business, technology changes including upgrades to compilers, database managers or other platform related upgrades; Impact Analysis, Estimating, Analysis, Coding, Unit Testing, System Testing, User Test Support and Documentation.

- Service Management – service planning, service measurement, reporting and control, service quality assurance and control, customer satisfaction and service evolution.

Actions speak louder than words. As a result of Capgemini's success with the MBCAReS, MBUSA continues to rely on Capgemini for new initiatives.

Benefits

Capgemini offers MBUSA the benefit of a strong delivery team on an international scale. MBUSA now benefit from Applications Management with greater:

- service reliability and flexibility of key systems;

- control on spending – freeing up funds and resources for business critical initiatives;

- access to top skills in today's IT market;

- ability to leverage in-house key resources.

The MBCAReS system improves relationships among the Mercedes-Benz retailers and is considered a prime example addressing the business-to-business (B2B) marketplace. Less time is now needed to review claims. Now they are processed once, decided on and accepted.

Also, emphasis has shifted away from increasing manpower to handle an increasing volume of claims. With MBCAReS there has been no increase in the number of claims staff, processing between 75,000 to 200,000 vehicles (more than double the volume).

MBUSA benefits from:

- overall reduction in application software maintenance and enhancement costs;

- continued high-quality support of mission-critical applications;

- increased delivery predictability – on time and within budget.

MBUSA can now better serve not only customers but also retailers, with more efficient claims processing and advantages in Accounts Receivable. Retailers can easily check into the system and better determine claims status, both from a standard and a policy point of view.

The Mercedes-Benz Manager of Strategic Client Systems commented that: 'Relying on consistent systems has greatly improved the quality of information that goes to production facilities, which enables us to improve the quality of the vehicles'.

'If it wasn't for the fact that Capgemini did the integration, we would have looked elsewhere for our AM support. The combination of integration and the 'insourcing' met our expectations – that we will have a high level of quality support and build relationships – in the user department here and in Germany.'

Written in co-operation with Mercedes-Benz USA LLC.

4.9

Ontario Power Generation

Adaptive outsourcing solution by Canada's OPG and Capgemini via New Horizon Systems Solutions

Upon full market liberalisation in the Canadian energy sector, Ontario Power Generation (OPG) needed to divest between 20 per cent and 65 per cent of its former generating capacity in order to comply with the new regulations.

OPG needed to reinvent itself in order to trade competitively in a new marketplace, and sought to leverage fixed costs of large scale IT systems across other companies. Following a detailed review of suppliers, OPG selected Capgemini as their chosen partner.

The strategy, announced by both partners via creation of a joint-venture – New Horizon System Solutions – has become one of the most innovative and truly adaptive outsourcing strategic partnerships to be found anywhere in the energy and utility marketplace, world-wide.

Client profile

In common with many other energy markets around the world, the Canadian power industry is in the process of large-scale liberalisation.

Ontario Power Generation (OPG) based in Canada's most populous province was part of a provincially-owned, former vertically-integrated monopoly. It is transforming itself in order to thrive in an open market environment, one in which new competitors are being encouraged to enter and provide a wider range of choice to consumers.

This new regulatory climate is bringing massive changes to all participants, both in their scale and in a sharp focus on being competitive. The former monopoly, Ontario Hydro, has already been separated into a power generation company (OPG), a power transmission and distribution business (Hydro One), and a systems operator (IMO).

Business issues

The first and most obvious challenge for OPG was that it was actually becoming smaller. This, in turn, meant that much of its infrastructure, both in terms of administrative processes and systems, was no longer relevant to the new reality. The former company possessed its own in-house IT and systems support, tasked with achieving efficiency for a massive utility business, where processes involved were complex and the scale of the operation was vast.

In the new marketplace, OPG is one of several potential competitors aiming to win business from consumers, now able to pick and choose their provider. In service terms, the emphasis for OPG was to move towards:

- building customer relationships;

- managing risk;

- facilitating wholesale trading;

- achieving higher standards of efficiency;

- enabling it to market new service offerings.

Above all, OPG needed to reduce costs. The administrative framework needed by OPG was clearly far too costly for a business regulated to become a much smaller, more market-driven and more agile business.

Management at OPG recognised that fixed costs invested in large scale IT systems could be better leveraged across other companies. In addition, since OPG was in the process of selling generation facilities, an external partner was required to operate OPG's systems and sell services to potential new owners of plants sold.

After reviewing a range of potential partners, OPG concluded that Capgemini had both the capability and the innovative approach needed to be its chosen partner.

Solution

The strategy, jointly agreed by OPG and Capgemini, was first announced some 18 months prior to full market liberalisation. It has become one of the most innovative and truly adaptive outsourcing strategic partnerships to be found anywhere in the energy and utility marketplace, world-wide.

The key to its success has been the inventive and aggressive determination shown by both partners to leverage the partnership not just to achieve efficiency gains on existing business (vital though this was) but to create a growing business for the future. The relationship was structured with this goal very much in mind. Key features of the plan included:

Setting up NHSS as a new company

Both parties set up a new company as a vehicle for IT outsource services. Known as New Horizon System Solutions (NHSS), the company was jointly owned, with Capgemini as the majority shareholder (51 per cent).

Outsourcing to NHSS

Former IT employees of OPG were offered employment at NHSS, which then agreed to supply service to OPG at an appropriate level. The level of the service had to be flexible, commensurate with OPG's changing business requirements brought upon by a reduction of its size in Ontario.

Outsourcing from NHSS

Consistent with the strategy, NHSS sold related IT outsourcing business to Bruce Power, new owners of the Bruce nuclear power facility. The latter had been sold by OPG under the terms of the new regulatory framework.

The key element of the approach, and the factor that takes it to a different level from standard outsourcing deals, is the way that both partners built service and financial incentives into the relationship from the outset. NHSS is challenged to achieve increased efficiency gains for delivery to its clients by a benefit-sharing contractual arrangement.

For OPG it means that a former fixed overhead cost is a potential source of continuous value-added benefit. For Capgemini, it creates a strategic partnership with a strong and fundamental incentive to seek cost reduction, jointly and mutually.

New Horizon Systems Solutions offers a vast range of application and infrastructure management solutions to their customers through pre-determined service level agreements (SLAs).

From an applications management development and support perspective, NHSS provides application portfolio management, maintenance, design, and user support services in areas such as finance, HR, work management and data warehousing. With over 500 staff, NHSS supports and develops on numerous systems and platforms including SAP, PeopleSoft, Indus Passport, web applications, B2B applications, Microsoft tools, middleware solutions and more.

NHSS also provides extensive IT infrastructure support and management via two state-of-the-art Data Centres with 24/7 monitoring and innovative disaster recovery configurations. Employees also support over 300 custom applications and serve 600 to 1,000 calls per day through their help-desks. From planning and infrastructure architecture to service and quality management, NHSS is a predominant infrastructure provider to the energy industry.

Benefits

The announcement of NHSS was greeted with great interest, both in the North American outsourcing market as well as in the global energy and utilities industry. The challenges faced by OPG, dealt with in innovative fashion through the NHSS approach, are virtually universal in their significance.

Large utilities all over the world are seeking ways to create value from the non-core and unreasonably large internal support functions. The partnership between OPG and Capgemini has created a model that has much to offer many other businesses. That model, however, is of its nature dynamic – change is constant.

OPG has now transferred its interest in NHSS entirely to Capgemini. OPG will remain NHSS' largest customer and continues to benefit from performance gains. NHSS has complete freedom to extend its services across the marketplace.

Customers of NHSS will see the power of a fully-integrated service from Capgemini's end-to-end solutions, ranging from strategy to process management and from applications management and infrastructure solutions to NHSS' separate service.

With emphasis on the energy and utilities sector, and with a working model based on truly adaptive outsourcing, this approach is proving hard to resist. Significant new contracts have followed OPG, and as the business grows, so the clients, themselves, continue to gain in terms of service efficiency and financial return from this increasingly strategic relationship.

NHSS has already extended its footprint in the energy industry to serve the IT requirements for not only a generation company, but also a transmission and distribution business.

The justification for an adaptive enterprise approach can be seen with stark clarity in market sectors world-wide. Commercial and regulatory changes, alike, make both an innovative vision and an adaptive approach a basic necessity in many different areas of business.

The New Horizon System Solutions story demonstrates how flexible outsourcing can be a key ingredient in helping large enterprises to transform themselves fast, efficiently and successfully into the competitive, agile businesses likely to be winners in the years ahead.

A senior member of OPG's management team illustrates real benefit of the partnership:

'OPG faced a critical business requirement at the outset - to shrink business operations, grow IT capabilities without a corresponding increase in technology support costs.'

'The direct result of this unique partnership with Capgemini is that we have divested about 65 per cent of our operations, turned a huge technology cost into a new revenue stream, and still saved about 20 per cent in IT costs.'

'We are delighted with a partnership that offers genuine value to all parties involved.'

Written in co-operation with Ontario Power Generation, Inc.

4.10

Prudential

IT outsourcing gives flexibility and cost savings at Prudential

In reviewing the costs of its IT service provider PruTech, Prudential, a UK insurance leader, chose to outsource key IT operations to Capgemini.

Under a new long-term contract, Prudential will realise cost savings and, equally vital, a move from a rigid cost burden to one able to adapt to changing needs.

Client profile

Prudential is one of the largest life assurance companies in the UK, with over six million individual customers and 3,500 company pension schemes.

Prudential plc, through its businesses in Europe, the US and Asia, provides products, services and fund management to many millions of customers around the world. Prudential's reputation for integrity, security and value-for-money products and services has been built over 150 years.

Business issues

While Prudential enjoyed high rates of profitable expansion into the new millennium, it also faced, in its home UK market, the same issues of competition and rapidly changing regulatory requirements as other financial services providers.

In particular, there was an immediate need to operate competitively and profitably within the new Stakeholder Pension regime. Legislation in force since the beginning of fiscal year 2001 has limited annual charges to one per cent of a policyholder's funds. Prudential and other financial service providers believed that the 'one per cent' concept would have an impact across a broad range of financial products and services and the reduction of operational IT costs was a key focus area.

As a result, Pru Tech initiated the market testing of its UK mainframe and mid-range services with an emphasis on reducing cost and achieving greater cost flexibility.

Solution

The resulting selection process led to the award of a five-year outsourcing contract to Capgemini. The contract was won against three other short-listed bids with a detailed and carefully costed plan to achieve savings on budgeted IT costs while maintaining, and where necessary enhancing, the existing very high service levels. The agreement included the transfer of some 90 Pru Tech IT staff and its data centre at Reading, UK, to Capgemini. Key factors in the Capgemini plan to deliver cost savings included:

- installing improved technology and a higher degree of automation through a technology transformation over the first 12–18 months of the five-year contract;

- achieving economies of scale through infrastructure consolidation and Capgemini's purchasing power;

- opening the data centre to other Capgemini customers while converting it to full 24x7 operation.

Cost flexibility was as important to Prudential as cost savings. Dynamism in the company's product range and in its channels to market means that IT support can never remain static. It must facilitate a fast response to increasing or decreasing needs in any given area of the business.

With its multi-client plans for the data centre, Capgemini could offer a clear capability to 'flex' resources as required. This was reflected in the commercial terms of the contract, which are based on cost per unit of processing – a 'pay as you go' approach that combines fairness to both parties with high flexibility.

To ensure ongoing service levels, a detailed agreement was drawn up involving the regular monitoring of some 90 quantitative performance measures.

There were several reasons for the final selection of Capgemini as IT partner:

- an impressive track record of running mission-critical outsourcing contracts for major corporations;

- enthusiastic current client references from the insurance, banking and other sectors;

- a specific and detailed bid that scored highly both for credibility and cost-effectiveness;

- a strong reputation on the human resources front for respecting the letter and spirit of TUPE (Transfer of Undertakings, Protection of Employment) requirements;

- a good cultural fit, evident from a number of assignments successfully carried out by Capgemini for the Prudential over the past 20 years.

Benefits

Prudential has confirmed that the benefits that will result from outsourcing are truly significant ones. The company believes:

'The contract with Capgemini secures the flexibility of cost that is vital when operating in an environment that changes as rapidly as financial services.

Fixed costs have been converted into variable costs and Prudential is now free to explore product and service innovations with the right level of IT support and expenditure.

Service levels, including such vital factors as availability and response times for the several systems involved, are being very carefully and objectively monitored and there is confidence that those levels will be maintained or enhanced.

The technical transformation has already started and, based on past experience of Capgemini's approach to project management, successful completion on schedule is expected.

There is great benefit in having access to Capgemini's pool of technical expertise so that it is now quicker and easier to deploy experts in many areas of IT, without the issues of recruitment in today's tight labour market.'

Written in co-operation with Prudential plc.

4.11

Sprint

Expanding leadership through applications management outsourcing

Sprint is a global communications company, serving 26 million business and residential customers in more than 70 countries.

Due to Sprint's success in the ever-growing telecommunications market, it decided to outsource specific areas of its business to Capgemini.

As a result, with more time to focus on its core competency, Sprint has been able to increase its flexibility and speed in the marketplace. Working with Capgemini provided Sprint with less risk, increased efficiency, and higher speed to market, giving it more flexibility in meeting its customers' needs.

Client profile

Sprint is a global communications company serving more than 26 million business and residential customers in over 70 countries. With approximately 80,000 employees world-wide and more than $26 billion in annual revenues, Sprint is widely recognised for developing, engineering, and deploying state-of-the-art network technologies, including the United States' first nationwide all-digital, fibre-optic network.

Sprint's award-winning Tier 1 internet backbone is being extended to key global markets to provide customers with a broad portfolio of scalable IP products. Sprint's high-capacity, high-speed network gives customers fast, dependable, non-stop access to the vast majority of the world's internet content. Sprint also operates the largest 100-per cent digital, nationwide PCS wireless network in the US, already serving the majority of the nation's metropolitan areas, including more than 4,000 cities and communities.

Sprint comprises the FON Group and the PCS Group – representing the company's wireline and wireless businesses. The FON Group operates Sprint's core wireline telecommunications operations, which include long distance; local telephone and product distribution; and directory publishing businesses.

Sprint announced a series of key strategic initiatives to continue to build Sprint PCS into a wireless powerhouse and transform Sprint's FON Group into a data-centric operation.

Business issues

The telecommunications industry is constantly evolving, and customer demand and technological innovation require the leading players to adapt and respond quickly.

Sprint's management recognised that its expanding leadership within the industry, coupled with rapidly rising consumer demand, meant that Sprint no longer chose to manage all aspects of its business internally.

At the same time, various business growth initiatives created a need within Sprint's Long Distance Division to engage the services of an outside supplier. Capgemini was selected to rapidly expand the development of software, support production, and complete capacity testing.

A primary requirement of this engagement was to free up key members of the leadership team to allow them to focus on Sprint's core competencies.

Solution

Capgemini's solution was to provide Sprint with one million project hours to address the following:

- *Technology Infrastructure and Operations:* Support Sprint's technology infrastructure on a 24x7 basis to effectively deliver the required capacity. Additionally, establish an efficient management structure to address administrative support, operations staffing, financial management, and facilities management.

- *Real Estate and Facilities:* Leverage Capgemini's proven experience with Application Development Centres to design and build specific facilities that will foster a high-performance environment – creating space on Sprint sites for business expansion.

- *Human Resources:* Structure Capgemini's staffing according to Sprint's competencies to promote adaptation and growth, in tandem with technologies and business needs. The focus was on retaining employees and developing subject matter expertise to be able to offer staff specialised skill sets.

The service packages provided were varied, but encompassed the entire systems lifecycle, including: analysis, design, development, testing, and implementation, as well as post-implementation and production support, technology transfers (new hardware or software platform), and supplemental resource staffing.

These centre-based services are being delivered primarily from Capgemini facilities in Chicago and Irvine, California, which are connected to Sprint's infrastructure. There is also an onsite component that includes resources working within Sprint facilities in Kansas City and Dallas.

Within the first eight months of the five-year contract, Capgemini identified, leased, designed, built, and provisioned two dedicated Application Development Centres for Sprint's use.

Capgemini successfully deployed 520 dedicated staff to the established development centres in less than nine months, and completed more than 200 client assigned projects in the first 12 months of the five-year project.

Benefits

The successful transition of applications, accompanied by consistent delivery, has provided Sprint with the ability to reposition its own critical resources to pursue strategic projects within its core competency.

The structured staffing approach enabled Sprint to increase its flexibility and speed in the marketplace. Having the ability to exchange resources meant that experts could be staffed quickly with no extra cost. Access to special skills at Capgemini has supported the transformation of Sprint – providing less risk, increased efficiency, and higher speed to market.

So seamless was this operation that Capgemini was recognised by Sprint as an extension of its organisation.

As customer demand increases, Sprint is well positioned to seize market share across many industry growth sectors. Sprint's confidence in Capgemini's ability to manage and improve elements of its business enables Sprint to retain a sharp focus on this demanding, yet exciting, marketplace.

Sprint's management sees the benefits of using Capgemini's Applications Management solution:

'Their persistence has contributed to the overwhelming positive response from our users, executives, and customers.'

'The project had a very aggressive schedule and challenging requirements. Capgemini stepped up to the challenge and met or exceeded all of the deadlines.'

Written in co-operation with Sprint Communications Company L.P.

Appendices

Transformational Outsourcing: Helping companies adapt to a volatile future

An IDC White Paper sponsored by Capgemini

The beginning of this century has witnessed some unforeseen business events – the Enron and WorldCom scandals, the crisis in Argentina, the fall of the NASDAQ exchange, and pillars of the business community closing their doors. Such events have led to massive uncertainty and instability in most markets.

During economic booms, consumers spend, investors lend, and businesses pop up and expand everywhere. The 'to-do' list of management is overwhelming and loaded with the details of growing a business. Alternatively, when the economy experiences a downturn, all eyes turn toward reducing expenses, leveraging existing investments, and gaining efficiency. Businesses in today's turbulent environment should consider creative strategies to help them weather the volatility in today's markets. One of these strategies is outsourcing.

Companies have been outsourcing various functions of their businesses – from call centres to networks to facilities management – for decades. And, given the growth of the overall outsourcing market, it's clear that the strategy is steadily gaining acceptance. Yet, there is an evolutionary change under way in the adoption of outsourcing services. In the past, businesses viewed outsourcing largely as a way to meet financial objectives. Therefore, tactical considerations, such as reducing costs, transforming fixed costs to variable, and liberating capital, were often the key reasons cited for turning to an outsourcing service provider.

But now companies face a more challenging business environment. It is more global, competitive, networked, and unpredictable. As a result, the decision to outsource is moving into the boardroom, and companies are relying on this strategy to transform their businesses. More customers are focusing on the core business, increasing flexibility, and achieving stronger financial performance, rather than simply relying on tactical cost-based reasons for outsourcing.

Study contents and topics

To gain better insight into the challenges and conditions of the business environment, the needs of the enterprise and how outsourcing can address these pressures, IDC conducted in-depth surveys of 65 senior decision-makers in large companies.

This paper examines the study findings, specifically as they relate to the volatility of the business environment, a company's need for flexibility, and how transformational outsourcing can help companies become adaptive and more successful. Specifically, this paper will discuss the following:

- companies' business challenges and industry volatility;

- the outsourcing market today;

- the future of outsourcing – transformational outsourcing;

- the changing nature of supplier and customer relationships;

- conclusion.

Business challenges

Changing customer demands, regulatory changes, and the need to cut costs are just some of the hurdles that businesses must face, and the current IDC study confirmed them. Figure 1 presents the respondents' answers when IDC asked executives to identify the challenges of their industries. Certainly, costs are top of mind these days.

However, we also see other less controllable events and factors that will undoubtedly impact organisations. Take the needs of customers, for instance. Regardless of one's business, chances are that customers have become more savvy and educated, as well as more demanding. Regulatory decisions are very likely out of executives' hands, yet these decisions can profoundly affect the way they conduct business. Mergers, acquisitions, and other consolidations may provide companies with scale and resources, but also integration complications in technological and intellectual capital.

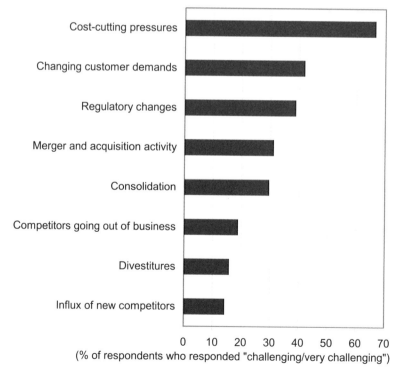

Figure 1 Business challenges

Not surprisingly, it appears that the top challenge in almost all vertical industries, with the exception of healthcare, is cost-cutting pressures (see Table 1). Within healthcare, regulatory mandates appear to be most pressing, no doubt due to the implications of the impending Health Insurance Portability and Accountability Act (HIPAA). In general, regulatory mandates and changing customer demands also received high rankings.

Table 1 Top challenges by vertical industry

Industry	Top Challenge
Consumer products, retail, distribution	Cost-cutting pressures
Energy, utilities, chemicals	Cost-cutting pressures
Financial services	Cost-cutting pressures, regulatory changes
Healthcare	Regulatory changes
Life sciences	Cost-cutting pressures, regulatory changes
Telecommunications, media, networks	Cost-cutting pressures, changing customer demands
Manufacturing	Cost-cutting pressures, competitors going out of business

When IDC segmented the responses by region, once again, cost-cutting pressures tops the list of challenges. There are subtle differences in the ranking of the various difficulties, as evidenced in Figure 2, possibly attributable to the fact that the European economy typically follows the path of the US economy six months later.

For instance, while Europe is now in the throes of an economic downturn, North America appears to be on the road to recovery. And while North American business saw massive consolidation last year, only 21 per cent of respondents in North American businesses indicated that consolidation was a considerable challenge compared with 45 per cent of the European respondents indicating that Europe is now in the midst of a consolidation phase.

Industry volatility

Regardless of a business' industry or geographic location, the challenges presented above are compounded by the fact that they are ongoing, unpredictable, and often unmanageable, making the overall business climate volatile and the need for adaptability paramount.

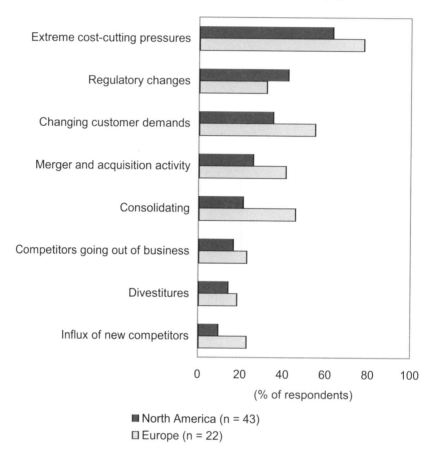

Figure 2 Business challenges by region

When IDC asked the survey respondents about the volatility of their industries, all seven industries indicated some level of environmental flux. Overall, almost two-thirds of the companies interviewed consider their industry to be volatile, and more than one-third of the companies believe that the volatility is permanent. The telecommunications, financial services, and energy/utilities/chemicals segments appear to be the most volatile (see Figure 3). Given the regulated nature of these segments and the rash of mergers and acquisitions, it is easy to understand why.

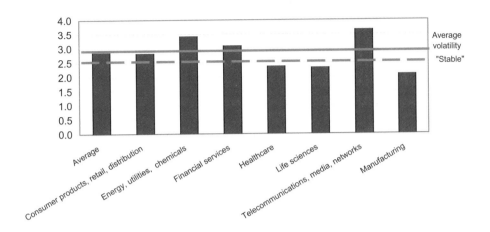

Figure 3 Volatility by industry

IDC contends that even though some industries might be relatively predictable today, no business is guaranteed a stable future. For instance, manufacturers will face added pressure from competitors – both domestically and from foreign firms – that can often produce the same goods cheaper and faster. Meanwhile, healthcare companies harbour lingering manual processes, and disparate systems create process inefficiencies. New regulatory constraints, such as HIPAA, are forcing healthcare organisations to make sweeping changes to address them. Savvy business executives in any industry should prepare their companies today to be adaptive and flexible tomorrow.

Outsourcing: where are we today?
Managing the unmanageable

If the future is unknown and the business environment continues to be in flux, exactly what can companies do to help manage the unmanageable? IT is certainly one way for companies to gain a competitive edge and address their business challenges. But technology changes at an astounding rate and is often not a company's core competency; thus, managing those technology changes becomes an added stress to running a company rather than a panacea. Furthermore, many companies invested tremendous resources in IT over the past few years and have yet to truly exploit its capabilities.

IDC contends that outsourcing is one way for businesses to ground their organisations in a sound strategy that resonates in any economic climate, bull or bear. This is evidenced by the continuous growth in the outsourcing market. IDC expects the IT outsourcing market to grow to $113 billion by 2006, representing a five-year compound annual growth rate (CAGR) of 12.3 per cent, and the business process outsourcing (BPO) market to reach $1.2 trillion by 2006. More than 88 per cent of enterprises surveyed in this study currently outsource a business or IT function, and 82 per cent of the companies interviewed have outsourced a core IT or business function over the past five years.

Outsourcing can reduce risks, optimise existing investments, and establish a sound, flexible IT strategy. In fact, the results of the current study indicate that companies in volatile industries are already embracing outsourcing as a way of managing uncertainty. As shown in Figure 4, companies in volatile industries have a greater than average tendency to outsource IT functions. And the trend is only expected to continue.

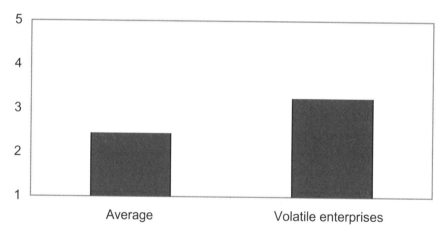

Figure 4 Tendency to outsource IT and business functions

Over the next five years, 77 per cent of the companies surveyed expect to outsource the same or more functions. Moreover, of companies that indicated that they outsource all or most IT functions, two-thirds characterise their industries as volatile and expect the level of volatility to continue indefinitely. This outlook underscores the importance of a sound underlying strategy that will support the fluctuating business conditions and needs (see Figure 5).

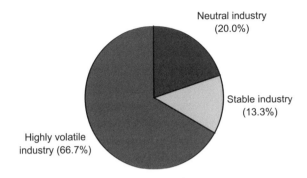

Note: Of those enterprises that "outsource heavily," nearly 67% would characterise their industry as highly volatile

Figure 5 Most of the enterprises that outsource characterise their industries as volatile

These same companies in dynamic industries – specifically financial services, energy/utilities/chemicals, and telecommunications – spend more than twice the average on outsourcing services, reinforcing this theory (see Figure 6). Other IDC research also indicates that these volatile industries spend more annually on services. According to IDC's Services Contracts Database, on average, companies spend $4.9 million on application outsourcing services, while those in the financial services, energy/utilities/chemicals, and telecommunications segments spend an average of $8.9 million per year. The difference appears to be less substantial among BPO spending; the overall average annual spending for these services is around $19 million, whereas the average for enterprises in the more volatile segment is $22.7 million (see Figure 7).

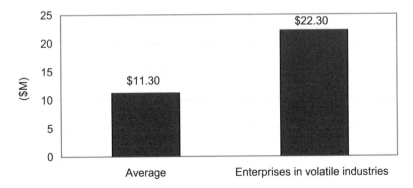

Figure 6 Annual spending on outsourced services

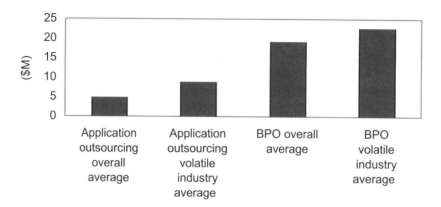

Figure 7 Annual spending on outsourcing

Why do companies outsource?

Traditionally, companies have outsourced for primarily tactical reasons. The most typical driver for outsourcing is to control expenses, but there have also been a number of other drivers for, and benefits of, outsourcing, including:

- faster and higher-quality service, improved efficiency;
- access to new skills and technology;
- staff reallocation;
- lower long-term capital investments;
- improved predictability of costs.

What do companies outsource?

Should business executives decide that outsourcing is right for their companies, the first fundamental question to ask is: 'What functions, processes, or systems am I comfortable outsourcing?' Figure 8 reveals the top areas that the survey respondents currently outsource. The findings are consistent with other IDC research studies.

More than half indicated that they turn to a service provider for application development. Outsourcing of the IT infrastructure was the second most common area to outsource, followed by payroll processing,

IT help desk, logistics, and customer contact centres. This list presents an interesting mix of both IT and business processes outsourcing; however, all of these areas are technology intensive, which confirms that companies tend to outsource highly technical and complex functions so that they can focus more clearly on their own business issues. Respondents indicated that they would continue to outsource these more technical and resource-intensive functions over the next several years.

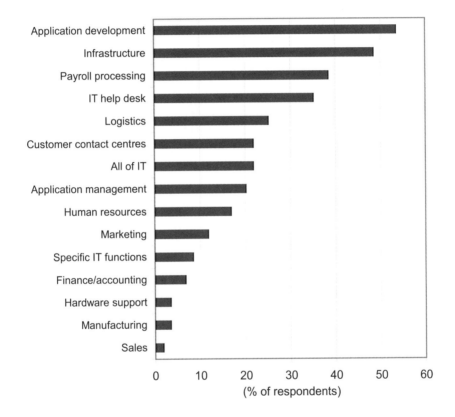

Figure 8 What do companies outsource?

There's no doubt that companies are relying more and more on technology to run their businesses, but managing and keeping up with the latest innovations can be dizzying. During prosperous years, a business might need the ability to ramp up and scale quickly. Meanwhile, during leaner times, an organisation may not have the internal resources necessary to carry out the IT of business functions. In either scenario, the outsourcing value proposition is flexible and adaptable and can alleviate these woes.

When segmented by verticals, slight differences appear in adoption of various outsourced functions. As shown in Table 2, application development was the number 1 function to be outsourced in the consumer products and retail, energy/utilities/chemicals, and manufacturing segments. For financial services and healthcare organisations, infrastructure topped the list of functions to outsource.

Telecommunications, media, and networks firms cited payroll processing as the number 1 area to outsource.

Table 2 Most commonly outsourced functions by vertical industry

Vertical	Function
Consumer products, retail, distribution	Application development
Energy, utilities, chemicals	Application development
Financial services	Infrastructure
Healthcare	Infrastructure
Life sciences	Application development
Telecommunications, media, networks	Payroll processing
Manufacturing	Application development, infrastructure

The evolution of business process outsourcing

One of the inhibitors to outsourcing of any flavour is the perceived loss of control. The more responsibility a company hands off to a third party, the greater this perception and fear. Thus, it is not surprising that in the current study findings, respondents are slightly less willing to outsource business functions than they are IT. Chances are, unless a company is in a high-tech field, IT is not its core competency. Executives understand the value of new technologies, and see IT outsourcing as a means to access it. For BPO, the decision is a bit more complicated. It's no longer just about outsourcing IT, but about transferring responsibility for the actual business function.

However, competitive pressures are compelling companies to rethink their BPO positions. Given the inhibitors and study findings, why is the BPO opportunity an order of magnitude larger than the IT outsourcing opportunity? Compared with the IT outsourcing market, the BPO services market, as a whole, is a relatively new and growing segment of outsourcing services. However, within BPO itself, the maturity of the concept varies across business functions. IDC has identified three levels of maturity for BPO adoption and acceptance. The three levels are as follows:

- *Emerging BPO segments*. For business functions, such as HR and procurement, BPO is a relatively new and emerging opportunity. In these areas, adoption rates are currently low but growth projections are high.

- *Well-established, but continually growing, BPO segments*. In other segments, such as logistics and customer care, BPO is hardly new. Nevertheless, the application of technology, competitive pressures, globalisation, and other factors are putting a new spin on BPO in these areas and, in turn, causing growth projections to be high.

- *Mature BPO segments with pockets of growth*. The third category comprises mature BPO segments such as facility operations, engineering, and legal services. For the most part, these are areas that companies outsource without batting an eye, simply because these functions are very specialised and few companies invest resources to have these capabilities internally (eg security services, legal services, building maintenance, janitorial services, infrastructure, and construction). One could argue that for these functions, companies generally do not really go through a strategic process of deciding whether to insource or outsource but that they have come to be accepted as the way of managing them.

Outsourcing: where do we go from here?

Our study findings confirm that outsourcing is steadily gaining acceptance in the business world and is used as a means to combat a host of challenges. More than 80 per cent of the enterprises agreed that they would spend the same or more on outsourcing services over the next three years. But perhaps these companies are looking for a new type of outsourcing – one that generates greater value for the enterprise.

Why will companies outsource in the future?

While the traditional outsourcing drivers and benefits are still prevalent and convincing in their own right, the market is undergoing an evolutionary change. Whereas five years ago, the motivators for outsourcing were 'cheaper, better, faster', the new mantra is 'better, cheaper, faster'. The increasing complexity and volatility of the business environment have compelled companies to evaluate their strategies, competencies, and resources and reassess the concept of outsourcing as a means to address their challenges and prepare their companies for the uncertain future.

When IDC asked large enterprises their reasons for outsourcing, executives cited their top three reasons as: focus on core business, reduce cost, and adapt to market conditions (see Figure 9). Certainly, cost is always going to be a factor in the decision-making process. But when asked their reasons for outsourcing assuming that cost is equal, executives responded differently. The top three reasons for outsourcing, assuming cost is equal, were ability to focus on core business, adaptability to market conditions, and ability to bring about a business transformation.

These findings confirm the belief that outsourcing is evolving from a tactical, cost-controlling mechanism to a strategic business move to change a company's business position. Although cost is still a factor with many organisations, given the challenges that most companies face and the volatility in many industries, businesses are viewing outsourcing in a whole new light, as a means to becoming more flexible and adaptable to rapidly changing business and market conditions. This progressive form of outsourcing is termed *transformational outsourcing*.

Transformational outsourcing: helping companies add value and reduce risk

Transformational outsourcing is defined as a long-term relationship through which a customer can leverage the entire ecosystem to both stimulate and facilitate continuous business change while achieving operational effectiveness.

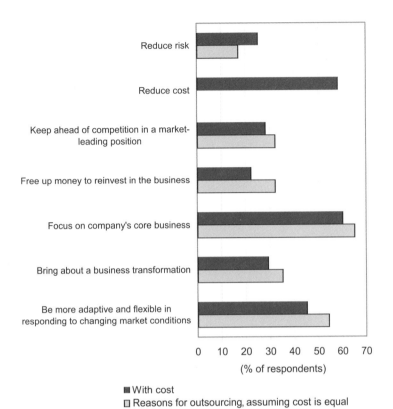

Figure 9 Drivers of outsourcing

Transformational outsourcing is a new way of looking at a familiar concept. Companies see outsourcing strategically – as a way of making a transformational business change – and some service providers are responding with new offerings and deal types. Table 3 highlights the fundamental differences between the two approaches.

Table 3 Traditional outsourcing versus transformational outsourcing

Traditional Outsourcing	Transformational Outsourcing
Tactical	Strategic
Operational focus	Business focus
Focus on cutting costs	Focus on creating value
Impose control	Manage uncertainty
Objective is to offload non-core functions	Objective is business change

When IDC asked executives about the benefits of transformational outsourcing, they cited more strategic gains like adaptability and flexibility (see Figure 10). These responses suggest that companies have a rather progressive view of this form of outsourcing. Looking beyond the typical reasons of staffing and cost, IT and business executives agreed that transformational outsourcing is intended to enhance a business's value and reduce risk by:

- *Enabling companies to focus on core competencies.* By handing over non-core activities to a trusted third party, a company can concentrate on activities central to its value proposition and increase its competitive positioning.

- *Helping to bring about a business transformation.* For companies in flux due to changing regulations, customer demands, or competitive dynamics, outsourcing enables even large enterprises to respond and change their business models more easily.

- *Providing greater flexibility and adaptability.* The flexibility gained through outsourcing helps a company react quickly to changing market conditions, fluctuating demand cycles, and increased competition.

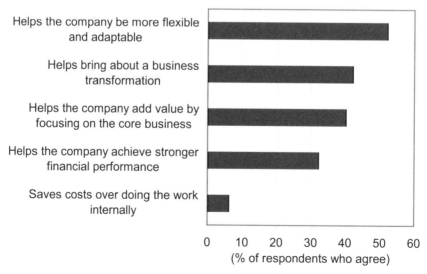

Figure 10 Benefits of transformational outsourcing

Transformational outsourcing and the technology adoption curve

While transformational outsourcing is still in its infancy, the early adopters of technology are already leading the pack toward a more strategic way of outsourcing. As shown in Figure 11, the companies to the far left of the technology adoption curve are those already embracing the concept of transformational outsourcing. Of those 'early adopters', 79 per cent agree that outsourcing is a way to transform their business. Cost will no longer be the major driver; businesses will outsource more of their non-core functions, freeing up money and resources to reinvest in their core business.

Since transformational outsourcing is only in the early adopter stage, in time IDC expects that it will become the norm. IDC found that those companies that are operating in volatile industries – financial services, energy/utilities/chemicals and telecommunications – are even more likely to adopt a transformational outsourcing relationship. Compared with an industry average of 72 per cent, 94 per cent of volatile companies see outsourcing as a way to be more flexible and adaptive in the marketplace (see Figure 12). Similarly, 83 per cent of volatile companies consider outsourcing as a way to bring about a transformational business change, compared with an industry average of 68 per cent (see Figure 13).

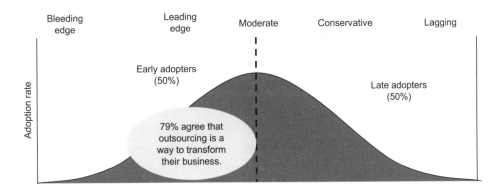

Figure 11 Transformational outsourcing and the technology adoption curve

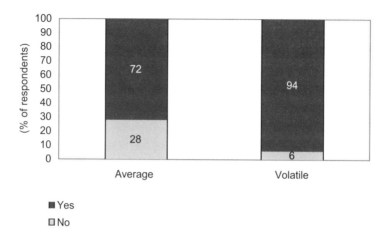

Figure 12 Impact of outsourcing on enterprises' flexibility and adaptiveness in the marketplace

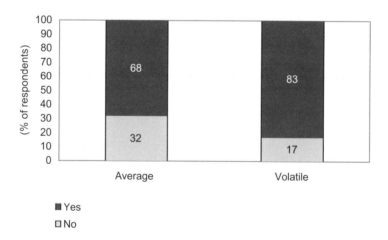

Figure 13 Impact of outsourcing on enterprises' ability to transform business

Not surprisingly, those companies in volatile industries are also 'early adopters'. As with most technologies or services, the early adopters are companies within the United States, often in the financial services or telecommunications industries. Once early adopters test the technology or service, European companies and enterprises within 'moderate or conservative' industries, such as healthcare, manufacturing, or life sciences, tend to adopt the technology or service about six months after the early adopters. IDC expects the adoption of transformational out-sourcing to follow a similar pattern.

Making the transformation: developing the right supplier relationships

The relationship between the service provider and the customer is evolving. As outsourcing becomes less tactical and more strategic, so must the nature of the relationship and contract change. In a transforma-tional outsourcing relationship, service providers are assuming more of the risk and taking a more active role in the relationship and the outcome.

Accordingly, customers are evaluating their service providers on much more than price. As shown in Figure 14, while price is a factor, it is not among the top reasons for working with one service provider over another. This finding is consistent with other IDC research studies. Customers find service and responsiveness, guaranteed uptime and availability, and industry expertise more important than price. Even more telling is that 70 per cent of customers are looking for a service provider that can help them enable their business strategies (see Figure 15). This is the key to a transformational or strategic outsourcing relationship.

Emerging trends in deal structures are further evidence of the progression. Contracts are moving to a risk-reward model, where the service provider is accountable for the ongoing performance and success of the solution. Rather than implementing a customer relation-ship management solution, billing the client, and hoping for the best, the service provider is assuming responsibility for the ongoing manage-ment of the application and infrastructure, thus sharing in the risk of something going wrong as well as the rewards of improved customer service and increased sales.

More than half of the enterprises indicated that they are looking for a trusted, strategic relationship with an outsourcer. This type of strategic relationship is a fundamental characteristic of transformational out-sourcing. A single strategic partner reduces the risk to the customer of engaging with multiple partners and suppliers and prevents the vendors from finger-pointing if something goes wrong. In this case, the transformational outsourcer assumes greater responsibility than a traditional supplier or service provider.

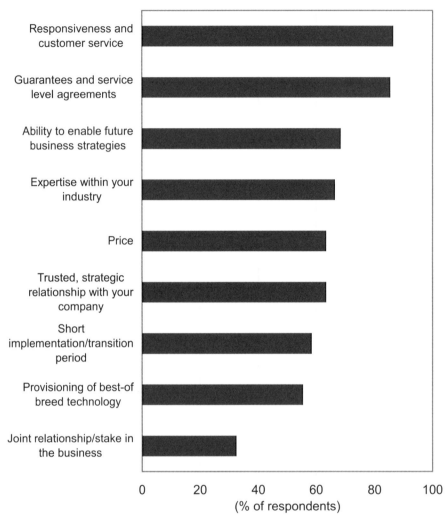

Figure 14 Characteristics enterprises look for in an outsourcing provider

As discussed, the right strategic outsourcing relationship can help businesses do more than save or manage costs. According to the research, a strategic outsourcing relationship can benefit a company by helping:

- the company focus on its core business;
- position the company to be more flexible and adaptable;
- the company achieve stronger financial performance;

- the company create shareholder value by freeing up money to reinvest in the business;

- the company bring about a business transformation.

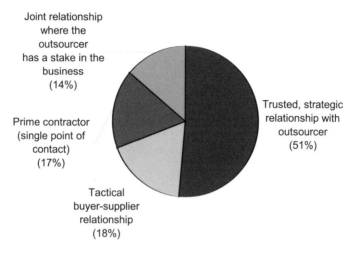

Figure 15 Enterprises are looking for a strategic relationship

In summary, regardless of what the future holds, outsourcing can prepare businesses to overcome challenges and open the door when opportunity knocks. Given volatility in many industries, businesses are viewing outsourcing in a whole new light – as a means to becoming more flexible and adaptable to rapidly changing business and market conditions.

Conclusion

The uncertainty that organisations face on a daily basis will undoubtedly bring about business issues and decisions that will require companies to take action. As executives attempt to chart the future of their companies, IDC encourages enterprises to take another look at outsourcing. Some of the world's most progressive companies are already there. Companies that do not at least consider the option may find themselves at a competitive disadvantage down the road. Even those companies in seemingly 'stable' industries should consider outsourcing because all industries, at one time or another, go through major changes. Whether the business is volatile or not, all companies will experience changes or challenges that lead them to consider transformational outsourcing as a way to address their pain points. In evaluating whether or not the business is ready for transformational outsourcing, consider the following questions:

- Is there pressure to focus on core competencies?
- Is the business expected to cut costs while improving service?
- Does the company need to free up money to invest in its core business?
- Are customers demanding more for less?
- Is the industry facing regulatory changes that could change the competitive nature of business?
- Is the organisation undergoing mergers and acquisitions requiring it to consider a flexible infrastructure?
- Does the business require comprehensive, integrated services?

Companies that answer yes to any of these questions may consider transformational outsourcing. Although this form of outsourcing may be off the beaten path right now, IDC suggests that enterprises in all industries begin reconsidering new ways to improve their bottom lines. Bull or bear markets, good times and bad, transformational outsourcing could be the one constant.

Appendix II

Capgemini locations

Asia-Pacific

(http://www.apc.capgemini.com/)

Australia

Sydney (Head Office)	Capgemini Level 4 50 Carrington Street Sydney NSW 2000	Phone: +61 (2) 9293 4000 Fax: +61 (2) 9293 4444
Adelaide	Capgemini Level 21 91 King William Street Adelaide SA 5000	Phone: +61 (8) 8233 6100 Fax: +61 (8) 8231 4998
Canberra	Capgemini 51 Allara Street Canberra ACT 2600 Australia	Phone: +61 (2) 6267 3962 Fax: +61 (2) 6246 1509
Melbourne	Capgemini Olderfleet Building Level 3477 Collins Street Melbourne VIC 3000	Phone: +61 (3) 9613 3000 Fax: +61 (3) 9613 3333

Austria

(http://www.at.capgemini.com)

Vienna	Capgemini Consulting Österreich AG Aspernbrückengasse 2 A-1020 Wien	Phone: +43 (1) 211 63 8400 Fax: +43 (1) 211 63 5000

Belgium

(http://www.be.capgemini.com)

Brussels (Head Office)	Capgemini Belgium N.V./S.A. Bessenveldstraat 19 B-1831 Diegem	Phone: +32 (2) 708 1111 Fax: +32 (2) 708 1110
Antwerp	Capgemini Atlantic House Noorderlaan 147 B-2030 Antwerp	Phone: +32 (3) 546 3111 Fax: +32 (3) 546 31 10
Hornu	Capgemini Rue de la Grande Campagne 6 B-7301 Hornu	Phone: +32 (65) 71 52 11 Fax: +32 (65) 71 52 00
Wavre Advanced Delivery Center	Capgemini Parc des Collines Rue Einstein 4 – Bâtiment E B-1300 Wavre	Phone: +32 (10) 23 66 11 Fax: +32 (10) 23 66 22

Canada

(http://www.ca.capgemini.com)

Calgary	Capgemini 440, 2nd Avenue, South West, Suite 800 Calgary, Alberta, T2P 5H2	Phone: +1 403 355 3700 Fax: +1 403 355 3701
Montreal	Capgemini C.P. 4555, succ B P.O. Box 4555, Stn B Montreal, Quebec H3B 4B5	Phone: 514 395 5800 Fax: 514 395 5801

Mississauga	Capgemini Canada P.O. Box 138, Suite 110090 Burnhamthorpe Road West Mississauga, Ontario L5B 3C3	Phone: 905 277 7300 Fax: 905 270 9984
Ottawa	Capgemini Canada P.O. Box 1507, Station B 360 Albert Street, Suite 810 Ottawa, Ontario K1R 7X7	Phone: 613 589 7474 Fax: 613 236 0116
Toronto	Capgemini Canada P.O Box 271 222 Bay Street, 25th Floor TD CentreToronto, Ontario M5K 1J5	Phone: 416 365 4400 Fax: 416 365 4401
Vancouver	Capgemini Canada Pacific Centre, P.O. Box 10092 700 West Georgia Street, Suite 1500 Vancouver, British Columbia V7Y 1C7	Phone: 604 678 4400 Fax: 604 678 4401

China

(http://www.cn.capgemini.com)

Czech Republic

(http://www.capgemini.cz)

Prague	Capgemini Czech Republic s.r.o. Růžová 14 110 00 Prague 1 Czech Republic	Phone: +420 2 24 50 5270 Fax: +420 2 24 50 5281

Denmark

(http://www.capgemini.dk)

Gentofte (Head Office)	Capgemini Danmark A/S Ørnegårdsvej 16 2820 Gentofte	Phone: +45 70 11 22 00 Fax: +45 70 11 22 01
Århus	Capgemini Danmark A/S Åhave Parkvej 31 8260 Viby J	Phone: +45 87 38 70 00 Fax: +45 87 38 70 01

Finland

(http://www.fi.capgemini.com)

Espoo (Head Office)	Capgemini Finland Niittymaentie 9 02200 Espoo	Phone: +358 (9) 452 651 Fax: +358 (9) 4526 5900
Espoo ADC Center	Capgemini Finland Niittymäentie 9 02200 Espoo	Phone: +358 (9) 452 651 Fax: +358 (9) 4526 5900
Helsinki	Capgemini Finland Fleminginkatu 34 F 00510 Helsinki	Phone: +358(9) 452 651 Fax: +358(9) 4526 7920
Helsinki	Capgemini Finland PL 230 00051 SONERA	Phone: +358 (20) 401 Fax: +358 (20) 406 0432
Helsinki ASE Center	Capgemini Finland Kiviaidankatu 2 B 00210 Helsinki	Phone: +358 (9) 278 4071 Fax: + 358 (9) 4526 7930
Lappeenranta	Capgemini Finland Laserkatu 8 53850 Lappeenranta	Phone: +358 (9) 452 651 Fax: +358 (9) 4526 7935
Tampere	Capgemini Finland Pyhajarvenkatu 5 C 33200 Tampere	Phone: +358 (9) 452 651 Fax: +358 (9) 4526 7933
Turku	Capgemini Finland Yliopistonkatu 14 20100 Turku	Phone: +358 (9) 452 651 Fax: +358 (9) 4526 7934
Espoo	Racap Solutions Piispantilankuja 4 02240 Espoo	Phone: +358 (9) 4526 5680 Fax: +358 (9) 4526 7910
Joensuu	Racap Solutions Torikatu 29 A 80100 Joensuu	Phone: +358 (9) 452 65 680 Fax: +358 (9) 4526 7931

France

(http://www.fr.capgemini.com)

Paris Siège social – Direction Générale France (Head Office)	Capgemini France 6-8, rue Duret 75784 Paris Cedex 16	Phone: +33 (0) 1 53 64 44 44 Fax: +33 (0) 1 53 64 44 45
Paris(Head Office)	Capgemini S.A. Place de l'Etoile 11 rue de Tilsitt 75017 Paris	Phone: +33 (0) 1 47 54 50 00 Fax: +33 (0) 1 42 27 32 11
Aix en Provence Network Infrastructure Services	Capgemini France Pavillon Martel, Domaine du Petit Arbois – BP 4513545 Aix en Provence cedex 04	Phone: +33 (0) 4 42 97 17 43 Fax: +33 (0) 4 42 97 17 30
Bayonne Life Science & Chemicals, Manufacturing, High Tech, Automotive	Capgemini France Cité du Palais Rue de Marhum 64100 Bayonne	Phone: +33 (0)5 59 25 34 00 Fax: +33 (0)5 59 34 01
Bordeaux Sud-Ouest	Capgemini France Parc d'Activité de Canteranne Bât. 3- 1er étage 33608 Pessac Cedex (Bordeaux)	Phone: +33 (0) 5 56 46 70 00 Fax: +33 (0) 5 56 36 16 90
Bordeaux Exploitation	Capgemini France Parc Cadéra – Immeuble Apollo Avenue Kennedy 33700 MERIGNAC	Phone: +33 (0) 5 57 92 70 50 Fax: +33 (0) 5 57 47 87 46
Brest Ouest	Capgemini France Z.I. de Kerscao 29480 Le Relecq-Kerhuon	Phone: +33 (0) 2 98 30 46 30 Fax: +33 (0) 2 98 30 46 20
Caen Ouest	Capgemini France 28 avenue Thies 14000 Caen (Brest)	Phone: +33 (0) 2 31 94 51 20 Fax: +33 (0) 2 31 93 49 83

Clermont-Ferrand Rhône-Alpes	Capgemini France Immeuble@number one Parc Technologique Pardieu 9, allée Evariste Galois 63170 Aubière	Phone: +33 (0) 4 73 28 23 81 Fax: +33 (0) 4 73 28 23 39
Grenoble Rhône-Alpes	Capgemini France 485, avenue de l'Europe Montbonnot 38334 SAINT-ISMIER Cedex	Phone: +33 (0) 4 76 52 62 00 Fax: +33 (0) 4 76 52 62 01
Le Mans Ouest	Capgemini France 2 allée des Gémeaux Centre Novaxis 72100 Le Mans	Phone: +33 (0) 2 43 57 45 00 Fax: +33 (0) 2 43 57 45 09
Lille Nord Est	Capgemini France Immeuble Vendôme-Flandre 20, rue du Ballon 59044 Lille cedex	Phone: +33 (0) 3 28 36 31 31 Fax: +33 (0) 3 28 36 31 32
Lille Exploitation	Capgemini France 839, avenue de la République 59700 Marcq-en-Baroeul	Phone: +33 (0) 3 28 36 30 20 Fax: +33 (0) 3 28 36 30 21
Lyon Rhône-Alpes & Centre de Formation	Capgemini France Immeuble Le Colysée 4-5 Place Charles Hernu, B.P. 2122 69603 Villeurbanne Cedex	Phone: +33 (0) 4 72 75 48 60 Fax: +33 (0) 4 72 75 48 99
Lyon Network Infrastructure Services	Capgemini France 13, rue des Émeraudes 69006 Lyon	Phone: +33 (0) 4 72 75 48 60 Fax: +33 (0) 4 78 24 61 70
Marseille Sud-Est	Capgemini France 90, chemin du Roy d'Espagne BP 23 13275 Marseille Cedex 09	Phone: +33 (0) 4 91 16 57 00 Fax: +33 (0) 4 91 25 00 58
Montpellier Sud-Est	Capgemini France Le Synergie 770, avenue Alfred Nobel 34000 Montpellier	Phone: +33 (0) 4 67 20 92 92 Fax: +33 (0) 4 67 20 92 93
Montpellier Systèmes Bancaires	Capgemini France Le Triade, Bât. II 215, rue Samuel Morse 34965 Montpellier Cedex 2	Phone: +33 (0) 4 67 20 64 90 Fax: +33 (0) 4 67 22 34 29

Mulhouse Nord Est	Capgemini France La Maison du bâtiment 12, allée Nathan Katz – BP 6046 68086 MULHOUSE Cedex	Phone: +33 (0) 3 89 36 33 66 Fax: +33 (0) 3 89 36 31 33
Nancy Nord Est	Capgemini France Centre d'Affaires Libération 101 avenue de la Libération – BP 20677 54063 Nancy Cedex	Phone: +33 (0) 3 83 95 85 85 Fax: +33 (0) 3 83 95 85 99
Nantes Ouest & Centre de Formation	Capgemini France 25 bis rue Paul Bellamy BP 81515 44015 Nantes cedex 01	Phone: +33 (0) 2 51 17 35 00 Fax: +33 (0) 2 51 17 35 10
Nantes Exploitation	Capgemini France Immeuble Salorges 2-Esc. B 3, boulevard Salvador Allende 44100 Nantes	Phone: +33 (0) 2 51 84 95 02 Fax: +33 (0) 2 40 69 65 01
NiceSud-Est & Centre de Formation	Capgemini France Porte de l'Arénas – Entree B 455, Promenade des Anglais 06200 Nice	Phone: +33 (0) 4 93 72 43 72 Fax: +33 (0) 4 93 21 02 95
Niort Ouest	Capgemini France 16 avenue Léo Lagrange 79000 Niort	Phone: +33 (0) 5 49 06 84 30 Fax: +33 (0) 5 49 06 84 39
Orléans Ouest	Capgemini France 12, rue Emile Zola4 5000 Orléans	Phone: +33 (0) 2 38 24 01 01 Fax: +33 (0) 2 38 54 54 98
Paris Finance	Capgemini France Coeur Défense Tour A – La Défense 4 110, esplanade du Général de Gaulle 92931 Paris La Défense Cedex	Phone: +33 (0) 1 49 67 30 00 Fax: +33 (0) 1 49 67 30 01
Paris Life Science & Chemicals, Manufacturing, High Tech, Automotive	Capgemini France Immeuble Elysées La Défense 7, place du Dôme 92056 Paris La Défense Cedex	Phone: +33 (0) 1 49 01 80 00 Fax: +33 (0) 1 49 01 74 24

Paris Institut	Capgemini France Tour Gamma A193, rue de Bercy 75582 Paris Cedex 12	Phone: +33 (0) 1 44 74 24 10 Fax: +33 (0) 1 43 47 24 24
Paris Infogérance	Capgemini FranceTour Anjou33, quai de Dion Bouton 92814 Puteaux Cedex (Paris)	Phone: +33 (0) 1 41 26 51 00 Fax: +33 (0) 1 41 26 51 01
Paris Energy, Utilities, Public Services	Capgemini France Coeur Défense Tour A – La Défense 4110, esplanade du Général de Gaulle 92931 Paris La Défense Cedex	Phone: +33 (0) 1 49 67 30 00 Fax: +33 (0) 1 49 67 30 01
Paris Consumer Products Retail Distribution (CPRD), Transport, Services	Capgemini France Immeuble Elysées La Défense 7, place du Dôme 92056 Paris La Défense Cedex	Phone: +33 (0) 1 49 01 80 00 Fax: +33 (0) 1 49 01 80 06
Paris High Growth & Middle Market	Capgemini France Coeur Défense Tour A – La Défense 4110, esplanade du Général de Gaulle 92231 Paris la défense Cedex	Phone: +33 (0) 1 49 67 30 00 Fax: +33 (0) 1 49 67 30 01
Paris Exploitation	Capgemini France 3 et 4, square Edouard VII 75441 Paris Cedex 09	Phone: +33 (0) 1 49 24 53 00 Fax: +33 (0) 1 49 24 54 51
Paris Information Systems management	Capgemini France 3 et 4, square Edouard VII 75441 Paris Cedex 09	Phone: +33 (0) 1 49 24 53 00 Fax: +33 (0) 1 49 24 53 01
Paris Network Infrastructure Services	Capgemini France 3 et 4, square Edouard VII 75441 Paris Cedex 09	Phone: +33 (0) 1 49 24 53 00 Fax: +33 (0) 1 49 24 54 49
Pau Sud-Ouest	Capgemini France Centre Helioparc 2, avenue Pierre Angot 64000 Pau	Phone: +33 (0) 5 59 84 12 23 Fax: +33 (0) 5 59 80 26 31

Rennes Ouest	Capgemini FranceTechnopole Rennes Atalante Beaulieu 3 Allée de la Croix des Hêtres CS 46412 35064 Rennes Cedex	Phone: +33 (0) 2 99 12 55 00 Fax: +33 (0) 2 99 12 55 99
Rennes Exploitation	Capgemini France 31 bis, rue des Landelles 35510 Cesson Sévigné	Phone: +33 (0) 2 23 35 40 10 Fax: +33 (0) 2 23 35 40 15
Rouen Exploitation	Capgemini France 42/44, rue Jeanne d'Arc 76000 – Rouen	Phone: +33 (0) 2 32 76 41 80 Fax: +33 (0) 2 32 76 41 89
RouenOuest	Capgemini France Parc de la Vatine 15, rue Pierre de Gennes – BP 181 76130 Mont Saint-Aignan	Phone: +33 (0) 2 35 12 20 20 Fax: +33 (0) 2 35 59 12 16
Strasbourg Nord Est & Centre de Formation	Capgemini France Espace Européen de l'Entreprise Immeuble H1 15, avenue de l'Europe 67300 Schiltigheim	Phone: +33 (0) 3 88 56 86 10 Fax: +33 (0) 3 88 56 86 19
Toulouse Sud-Ouest & Centre de Formation	Capgemini France Technopolis 8, rue Paul Mesplé, B.P. 1155 31036 Toulouse Cedex	Phone: +33 (0) 5 61 31 52 00 Fax: +33 (0) 5 61 31 53 85
Toulouse Exploitation	Capgemini France 2 ter, rue Marcel Doret 31700 Blagnac (Toulouse)	Phone: +33 (0) 5 34 60 60 40 Fax: +33 (0) 5 61 30 08 59
Tours Ouest	Capgemini France 4 bis, rue Emile Zola 37000 Tours	Phone: +33 (0) 2 47 60 67 60 Fax: +33 (0) 2 47 60 67 69
Grenoble	Capgemini S.A. 3 rue Malakoff – BP 206 38005 Grenoble Cedex 1	Phone: +33 (0) 4 76 59 63 00 Fax: +33 (0) 4 76 51 53 20
Paris	Capgemini Service Place de l'Etoile 11, rue de Tilsitt 75017 Paris	Phone: +33 (0) 1 47 54 50 00 Fax: +33 (0) 1 47 27 32 11

Paris	Capgemini Telecom Media & Networks France Tour EUROPLAZA 20 ave. André Prothin 92927 La Défense Cedex	Phone: +33 (0) 1 49 00 40 00 Fax: +33 (0) 1 47 78 45 52
Paris	Capgemini Telecom S.A. 76 Avenue Kléber 75784 Paris Cedex 16	Phone: +33 (0) 1 47 54 52 00 Fax: +33 (0) 1 47 54 52 70
Paris	Capgemini Université Rue du Nid de Geai 78910 Béhoust-Orgerus	Phone: +33 (0) 1 30 88 38 38 Fax: +33 (0) 1 30 88 38 00
Paris	Gemini Telecom & Entertainment France Tour Europlaza 20, rue andré Prothin 92927 Paris La Défense Cedex	Phone: +33 (0) 1 49 00 20 00 Fax: +33 (0) 1 49 00 21 99
Rennes	Telecom Media & Entertainment Zirst Rennes Atalante 5 Allée de la Croix des Hêtres C.S. 50801 35018 Rennes Cedex	Phone: +33 (0) 2 99 27 45 45 Fax: +33 (0) 2 99 27 45 35

Germany

(http://www.de.capgemini.com)

Berlin (Head Office)	Capgemini Deutschland GmbH Neues Kranzler Eck Kurfürstendamm 21 D-10719 Berlin	Phone: +49 (0) 30 88 703 0 Fax: +49 (0) 30 88 703 111
Düsseldorf	Capgemini Deutschland GmbH Hamborner Strasse 55 D-40472 Düsseldorf	Phone: +49 (0) 211 470 68 0 Fax: +49 (0) 211 470 68 111
Frankfurt-Sulzbach	Capgemini Deutschland GmbH Am Limespark 2 D-65843 Sulzbach	Phone: +49 (0) 6196 999 0 Fax: +49 (0) 6196 999 11 11
Hamburg	Capgemini Deutschland GmbH Lübecker Strasse 1 D-22087 Hamburg	Phone: +49 (0) 40 2 53 18 0 Fax: +49 (0) 40 2 53 18 111
Hannover	Capgemini Deutschland GmbH Hackethalstr. 7 D-30179 Hannover	Phone: +49 (0) 511 67 82 700 Fax: +49 (0) 511 67 82 701

Köln	Capgemini Deutschland GmbH Konrad-Adenauer-Ufer 37 D-50668 Köln	Phone: +49 (0) 221 91 26 44 0 Fax: +49 (0) 221 91 26 44 30
München ASE Center	Capgemini Deutschland GmbH Karl-Hammerschmidt-Strasse 32 D-85609 Dornach b. München	Phone: +49 (0) 89 94 00 22 00 Fax: +49 (0) 89 94 00 22 22
München	Capgemini Deutschland GmbH Carl-Wery-Str. 42 D-81739 München	Phone: +49 (0) 89 94 00 0 Fax: +49 (0) 89 94 00 11 11
Stuttgart	Capgemini Deutschland GmbH Löffelstraße 44-46 D-70597 Stuttgart	Phone: +49 (0) 711 50 50 5 0 Fax: +49 (0) 711 50 50 5 333
Walldorf	Capgemini Deutschland GmbH Altrottstrasse 31 D-69190 Walldorf	Phone: +49 (0) 6227 73 39 00 Fax: +49 (0) 6227 73 39 39
Essen	Capgemini Systems GmbH Rellinghauser Strasse 37 D-45128 Essen	Phone: +49 (0) 201 8126 0 Fax: +49 (0) 201 8126 2557
Rüsselsheim	Capgemini Systems GmbH Eisenstrasse 3 D-65428 Rüsselsheim	Phone: +49 (0) 6142 60 34 0 Fax: +49 (0) 6142 60 34 102
Hamburg	sd&m Software Design & Management AG Lübecker Strasse 1D-22087 Hamburg	Phone: +49 (0) 40 25 44 91 01 Fax: +49 (0) 40 25 44 91 11
München	sd&m Software Design & Management AG Carl-Wery-Str. 42 D-81739 München	Phone: +49 (0) 89 638 12 0 Fax: +49 (0) 89 638 12 150
Offenbach	sd&m Software Design & Management AG Herrnstrasse 57 D-63065 Offenbach am Main	Phone: +49 (0) 69 829 01 0 Fax: +49 (0) 69 829 01 200
Ratingen	sd&m Software Design & Management AG Am Schimmersfeld 7a D-40880 Ratingen	Phone: +49 (0) 2102 99 57 0 Fax: +49 (0) 2102 99 57 50

Stuttgart	sd&m Software Design & Management AG Löffelstraße 46 D-70597 Stuttgart	Phone: +49 (0) 711 78 324 0 Fax: +49 (0) 711 78 324 150
Troisdorf	sd&m Software Design & Management AG Mühlheimer Strasse 3-7 D-53840 Troisdorf	Phone: +49 (0) 2241 97 37 0 Fax: +49 (0) 2241 97 37 222

Hungary

(http://www.capgemini.hu)

Budapest	Capgemini Hungary Puskás Tivadar utca 4. 2040 Budaörs	Phone: +36 23 506 800 Fax: +36 23 506 801

India

(http://www.in.capgemini.com)

Ireland

(http://www.ie.capgemini.com)

Dublin Application Product Intl	Capgemini Ireland Ltd International House 20–22, Lower Hatch Street Dublin 2	Phone: +353 1661 3266 Fax: +353 1661 4916

Italy

(http://www.it.capgemini.com)

Roma (Head Office)	Capgemini Italia Via di Torre Spaccata 140 00169 Roma	Phone: +39 06 231 901 Fax: +39 06 232 692 18
La Spezia	Capgemini Italia Via delle Pianazze 74 19136 La Spezia	Phone: +39 0187 98 451 Fax: +39 0187 98 45228
Milano	Capgemini Italia Viale Stendhal, 34 20144 Milano	Phone: +39 02 42261 Fax: +39 02 42262500
Napoli	Capgemini Italia Centro Direzionale – Isola G6 Int. 16/C – Via Giovanni Porzio, 480143 Napoli	Phone: +39 081 6068911 Fax: +39 081 787 98 80

Siracusa	Capgemini Italia Via Adda 9 sc.F 96100 Siracusa	Phone: +39 (0931) 463 564 15 Fax: +39 (0931) 463 564
Torino	Capgemini Italia I portici del lingotto Via Nizza 262 int.27 10126 Torino	Phone: +39 011 65 38 11 Fax: +39 011 65 38 1400

Japan

(http://www.capgemini.co.jp)

Tokyo	Capgemini KDDI Otemachi Building 1-8-1, Otemachi 1-chome, Chiyoda-ku, Tokyo Japan 100-0004	Phone: + 81 (3) 3279 9210 Fax: +81 (3) 3279 9211

Luxembourg

(http://www.lu.capgemini.com/)

Bertrange	Capgemini Luxembourg S.A. rue de Luxembourg, 295 L-8077 Bertrange	Phone: +(352) 44 04 98 1 Fax: +(352) 44 04 98 38

Malaysia

Kuala Lumpur	Capgemini Level 28 Tower 2 PETRONAS Twin Towers Kuala Lumpur City Centre 50088 Kuala Lumpur Malaysia	Phone: +60 (3) 2163 6800 Fax: +60 (3) 2163 1188

Mexico

(http://www.mx.capgemini.com)

MéxicoMéxico	Capgemini México Av. Guillermo González Camarena 1600 3er Piso Colonia Centro de Ciudad Santa Fe México, D.F. 01210	Phone: + 52 (55) 85 03 24 39 Fax: + 52 (55) 85 03 24 67

Netherlands

(http://www.nl.capgemini.com)

Utrecht (Head Office)	Capgemini Nederland B.V. Papendorpseweg 100 3528 BJ Utrecht P.O. Box 2575 3500 GN Utrecht The Netherlands	Phone: +31 30 689 89 89 Fax: +31 30 689 99 99
Utrecht	Capgemini Outsourcing B.V. Daltonlaan 300 3584 BK Utrecht P.O. Box 2575 3500 GN Utrecht The Netherlands	Phone: +31 30 689 44 22 Fax: +31 30 689 44 80

Norway

(http://www.no.capgemini.com)

Oslo (Head Office)	Capgemini Office address: Hoffsveien 1D, 0275 Oslo Mailing address: Pb. 475, Skøyen 0214 Oslo	Phone: +47 2412 8000 Fax: +47 2412 8001
Aandalsnes	Capgemini Strandgata 6 6300 Aandalsnes	Phone: +47 24 12 80 00 Fax: +47 24 12 71 03
Bergen	Capgemini Postboks 3950, Dreggen 5835 Bergen	Phone: +47 24 12 80 00 Fax: +47 55 90 66 01
Fredrikstad	Capgemini Kråkerøyvn. 2 1671 Kråkerøy	Phone: +47 24 12 80 00 Fax: +47 69 35 68 01
Trondheim	Capgemini Beddingen 10 7014 Trondheim	Phone: +47 24 12 80 00 Fax: +47 73 84 60 01
Stavanger	Capgemini Norge A.S Maskinveien 24, 4033 Stavanger	Phone: +47 24 12 80 00 Fax: +47 51 44 62 01

Poland

(http://www.pl.capgemini.com)

Warsaw (Head Office)	Capgemini Polska Sp. z o.o. Al. Jana Pawła II 12 00-124 Warsaw	Phone: + 48 22 850 92 00 Fax: + 48 22 850 92 01
Kraków Business Process Outsourcing Center	Capgemini Polska Sp. z o.o. – Oddział w Krakowie Ul. Lubicz 23 31-503 Kraków	Phone: + 48 12 631 63 00 Fax: + 48 12 629 60 61
Wrocław NearShore Center	Capgemini Polska Sp. z o.o. – Oddział we Wrocławiu Pl. Dominikański 3 50-159 Wrocław	Phone: +48 71 344 95 50 Fax: +48 71 344 95 58

Portugal

(http://www.pt.capgemini.com)

Lisboa (Head Office)	Capgemini Edifício Torre de Monsanto Lugar de Romeiras Miraflores 1495-046 Algés	Phone: +351 21 412 22 00 Fax: +351 21 412 22 99
Porto	Capgemini Edifício Cristal d'Ouro Rua do Campo Alegre, 830 – 8° Sala 374150 – 171 Porto	Phone: +351 22 608 06 60 Fax: +351 22 608 06 89

Romania

Bucharest	Gemini Consulting Str. Pache Protopopescu, Nr 60 Sector 2, Bucharest 70 334	Phone: +40 (1) 92 655 101/ 102 Fax: +40 (1) 252 7561

Singapore

Singapore sales.sg@ capgemini.com	Capgemini 10 Ang Mo Kio Street 65 #03-14/16 TechPoint Singapore 569059	Phone: +65 6484 3188 Fax: +65 6484 0172

Slovakia

(http://www.sk.capgemini.com)

Bratislava	Capgemini Slovensko, s.r.o. Zelezniciarfka 13 81 104 Bratislava	Phone: +42 12 444 55 678 Fax: +42 12 444 55 680

Spain

(http://www.es.capgemini.com)

Barcelona	Capgemini Avinguda Diagonal 640 08017 Barcelona	Phone: +34 (93) 495 86 00 Fax: +34 (93) 495 87 71
Madrid	Capgemini Anabel Segura, 14 Arroyo de La Vega 28100 Alcobendas Madrid	Phone: +34 (91) 657 70 00 Fax: +34 (91) 661 20 19

Sweden

(http://www.se.capgemini.com)

Fagersta	Capgemini Sweden Box 503 Björnbacksvägen 1 737 25 Fagersta	Phone: +46 (8) 5368 5000 Fax: +46 (223) 159 39
Göteborg	Capgemini Sweden Mölndalsvägen 36–38 412 63 Göteborg	Phone: +46 (8) 5368 5000 Fax: +46 (8) 5368 5301
Kalmar	Capgemini Sweden Varvsholmen 392 30 Kalmar	Phone: +46 (8) 5368 5000 Fax: +46 (480) 49 66 61
Karlshamn	Capgemini Sweden Södra Fogdelyckegatan 28 374 36 Karlshamn	Phone: +46 (8) 5368 5000 Fax: +46 (454) 32 59 51
Karlskrona	Capgemini Sweden Campus Gräsvik 2 371 75 Karlskrona	Phone: +46 (8) 5368 0000 Fax: +46 (545) 568 51
Linköping	Capgemini Sweden Box 483 S:t. Larsgatan 3 581 05 Linköping	Phone: +46 (8) 5368 5000 Fax: +46 (13) 14 24 31

Luleå	Capgemini Sweden Box 905 Kungsgatan 5 971 27 Luleå	Phone: +46 (8) 5368 5000 Fax: +46 (920) 872 33
Malmö	Capgemini Sweden Box 4032 Baltzarsgatan 31 203 11 Malmö	Phone: +46 (8) 5368 5000 Fax: +46 (8) 5368 3801
Stockholm	Capgemini Sweden Box 825 Gustavslundsvägen 131 161 24 Bromma	Phone: +46 (8) 5368 5000 Fax: +46 (8) 5368 5555
Sundsvall	Capgemini Sweden Box 875 Kolvägen 15 851 24 Sundsvall	Phone: +46 (8) 5368 5000 Fax: +46 (60) 594 702
Växjö	Capgemini Sweden Arabygatan 11 352 46 Växjö	Phone: +46 (8) 5368 5000 Fax: +46 (470) 74 79 61
Örebro	Capgemini Sweden Box 964 Norrbackavägen 7 701 32 Örebro	Phone: +46 (8) 5368 5000 Fax: +46 (19) 611 59 69

Switzerland

(http://www.ch.capgemini.com)

Zürich (Head Office)	Capgemini Schweiz Leutschenbachstrasse 95 8050 Zürich Switzerland	Phone: +41 (0) 1 560 24 00 Fax: +41 (0) 1 560 25 00
Basel	Capgemini Messeplatz 10/12 CH-4058 Basel Switzerland	Phone: +41 (0) 61 692 08 42 Fax: +41 (0) 61 692 08 50
Genf	Capgemini 12, avenue des Morgines CH-1213 Petit Lancy Switzerland	Phone: +41 (0) 22 879 52 00 Fax: +41 (0) 22 879 52 39

| Lausanne | Capgemini Suisse SA
Chemin du Viaduc 1
Postfach 272
CH-1000 Lausanne 16 Malley
Switzerland | Phone: +41 (0) 21 620 71 00
Fax: +41 (0) 21 620 71 99 |

United Kingdom

(http://www.uk.capgemini.com)

Woking Registered Office (Head Office)	Capgemini UK Woking (No. 1) Forge End, Woking, Surrey GU21 6DB	Phone: +44 (0) 1483 764 764 Fax: +44 (0) 1483 786 161
Birmingham	Capgemini UK 1 Avenue Road Aston Birmingham B6 4DU	Phone: +44 (0) 121 333 3536 Fax: +44 (0) 121 333 3308
Bristol	Capgemini UK Aztec Centre Aztec West Almondsbury Bristol BS32 4TD	Phone: +44 (0) 1454 626 626 Fax: +44 (0) 1454 893 030
Bristol	Capgemini UK Toltec Unit 1120 Park Avenue Aztec West Almonsbury Bristol BS32 4SX	Phone: +44 (0) 1454 873 933 Fax: +44 (0) 1454 873 636
Dublin	Capgemini UK International House, Lower Hatch Street, Dublin 2 Ireland	Phone: +353 1 639 0100 Fax: +353 1 639 0199
Edinburgh	Capgemini UK 36 South Gyle Crescent South Gyle Edinburgh Scotland EH12 9EB	Phone: +44 (0) 131 339 9339 Fax: +44 (0) 131 200 3700

Glasgow	Capgemini UK Regent Court 70 West Regent Street Glasgow Scotland G2 2QZ	Phone: +44 (0) 141 331 0414 Fax: +44 (0) 141 353 5858
Inverness	Capgemini UK c/o Scottish Hydro Electric 10 Henderson Road Inverness Scotland IV1 1AU	Phone: +44 (0) 1463 238 434 Fax: +44 (0) 1463 643 088
London	Capgemini UK 95 Wandsworth Road London SW8 2HG	Phone: +44 (0) 207 735 0800 Fax: +44 (0) 207 917 4666
London	Capgemini UK Capgemini House 76 Wardour Street London W1F 0UU	Phone: +44 (0) 20 7734 5700 Fax: +44 (0) 20 7297 3900
Nairn 1	Capgemini UK VERTEX Unit 9 Balmakeith Business Park Nairn IV12 5QR	Phone: +44 (0) 1667 458 008 Fax: +44 (0) 1667 458 040
Newcastle (Wynyard Park)	Capgemini UK Samsung Avenue Wynyard Billingham TS22 5TA	Phone: +44 (0) 1740 645 500 Fax: +44 (0) 1740 646 566
Rotherham	Capgemini UK PO Box 21 Aldwarke Lane Rotherham South Yorkshire S65 3SQ	Phone: +44 (0) 1709 710 071 Fax: +44 (0) 1709 846 229
Sale	Capgemini UK Capgemini House 77–79 Cross Street Sale Cheshire M33 7HG	Phone: +44 (0) 161 969 3611 Fax: +44 (0) 161 973 9016

Swansea	Capgemini UK Conwy House Tawe Business Village Castle Court Pheonix Way Swansea Enterprise Park Swansea SA7 9LA	Phone: +44 (0) 1792 792 777 Fax: +44 (0) 1792 792 666

United States

(http://www.us.capgemini.com)

New York (Head Office)	Capgemini U.S. 5 Times Square New York, NY 10036	Phone: +1 (917) 934 8000 Fax: +1 (917) 934 8001
Herndon (VA)	Capgemini Government Solutions LCC 2250 Corporate Park Drive Suite 410 Herndon VA 20171	Phone: +1 (571) 336 1600 Fax: +1 (571) 336 1700
Atlanta	Capgemini U.S.10 Glenlake Parkway, Suite 1000 Atlanta, GA 30328	Phone: +1 (404) 806 4200 Fax: +1 (404) 806 4850
Cambridge	Capgemini U.S. 600 Memorial Drive, Suite 100 Cambridge, MA 02139	Phone: +1 (617) 768 5400 Fax: +1 (617) 768 5402
Cambridge (ASE)	Capgemini U.S. 600 Memorial Drive, Suite 100 Cambridge, MA 02139	Phone: +1 (617) 768 5600 Fax: +1 (617) 768 577 7801
Charlotte	Capgemini U.S. 525 North Tryon Street Suite 1700 Charlotte, NC 28202	Phone: +1 (704) 331 6512 Fax: +1 (704) 805 7040
Chicago	Capgemini U.S. Santa Fe Center 224 S. Michigan Avenue, Suite 1500 Chicago, IL 60604	Phone: +1 (312) 356 3000 Fax: +1 (312) 356 2180
Chicago	Capgemini U.S. 111 North Canal, 15th Floor Chicago, IL 60606	Phone: +1 (312) 395 5000 Fax: +1 (312) 395 5001

Chicago (Rosemont)	Capgemini U.S. 10255 W. Higgins Road 3rd Floor Rosemont, IL 60018	Phone: +1 (312) 395 8000 Fax: +1 (312) 395 8001
Cincinnati	Capgemini U.S. River Center II 100 East River Center Boulevard Suite 500 Covington, KY 41011	Phone: +1 (859) 655 1500 Fax: +1 (859) 655 1501
Clark (NJ)	Capgemini U.S. 100 Walnut Avenue Clark, NJ 07066	Phone: +1 (732) 669 6000 Fax: +1 (732) 669 6205
Clayton	Capgemini U.S. The Plaza in Clayton 190 Carondelet Plaza, Suite 1200 Clayton, MO 63105	Phone: +1 (314) 290 8000 Fax: +1 (314) 290 8001
Cleveland	Capgemini U.S. 1200 Skylight Office Tower 1660 West Second Street Cleveland, OH 44113	Phone: +1 (216) 583 3300 Fax: +1 (216) 583 8319
Cupertino	Capgemini U.S. 20425 Stevens Creek Boulevard Cupertino, CA 95014-2261	Phone: +1 (408) 850 5500 Fax: +1 (408) 850 5501
Dallas	Capgemini U.S. 7701 Las Colinas Ridge One Panorama Center, Suite 600 Irving, TX 75063	Phone: +1 (972) 556 7000 Fax: +1 (972) 556 7001
Denver	Capgemini U.S. 4600 S. Syracuse Street, 9th Floor, Suite 963 Denver, CO 80237	Phone: +1 (303) 256 6575 Fax: +1 (303) 256 6576
Detroit	Capgemini U.S. 500 Woodward Suite 1620 Detroit, MI 48226	Phone: +1 (313) 887 1400 Fax: +1 (313) 887 1401
El Segundo	Capgemini U.S. 200 North Sepulveda Boulevard Suite 1000 El Segundo, CA 90245	Phone: +1 (310) 727 8400 Fax: +1 (310) 727 8848

Freehold (NJ)	Capgemini U.S. 3 Paragon Way Freehold, NJ 07728	Phone: +1 (732) 358 8900 Fax: +1 (732) 358 8801
Houston	Capgemini U.S. 1401 McKinney Street Suite 900 Houston, TX 77010	Phone: +1 (281) 220 5000 Fax: +1 (281) 220 5001
Irvine	Capgemini U.S. 18101 Von Karman Avenue Suite 400 Irvine, CA 92612	Phone: +1 (949) 567 8700 Fax: +1 (949) 567 8701
Kansas City (Service Center)	Capgemini U.S. 3315 North Oak Trafficway Kansas City, MO 64116	Phone: +1(816) 459 6000 Fax: +1 (816) 459 6333
Leawood	Capgemini U.S. 11300 Tomahawk Creek Parkway Suite 340 Leawood, KS 66211	Phone: +1 (913) 319 8000 Fax: +1 (913) 319 8001
Lyndhurst (Meadowlands)	Capgemini U.S. 1280 Wall Street West Lyndhurst, NJ 07071	Phone: +1 (201) 777 9100 Fax: +1 (201) 777 9101
Minneapolis/ St. Paul	Capgemini U.S. 220 South Sixth Street Suite 1200, South Tower Minneapolis, MN 55402	Phone: +1 (612) 492 2700 Fax: +1 (612) 492 2701
Minnetonka	Capgemini U.S. 5450–5485 Feltl Road, Suite 5478 Minnetonka, MN 55343	Phone: +1 (952) 908 3600 Fax: +1 (952) 908 3661
New York	Capgemini U.S. 750 Seventh Avenue New York, NY 10019	Phone: +1 (212) 314 8200 Fax: +1 (212) 314 8202
New York (ADC)	Capgemini U.S. 55 Broad Street New York, NY 10004	Phone: +1 (917) 320 3200 Fax: +1 (917) 320 3201
New York (ASE)	Capgemini U.S. 55 Broad Street New York, NY 10004	Phone: +1 (917) 320 3100 Fax: +1 (917) 320 3101

Philadelphia	Capgemini U.S. Two Commerce Square Suite 4000 2001 Market Street Philadelphia, PA 19103-7096	Phone: +1 (267) 336 3600 Fax: +1 (267) 336 3601
Phoenix	Capgemini U.S. One Renaissance Square 2 North Central Ave.; Suite 2600 Phoenix, AZ 85004	Phone: +1 (602) 462 8800 Fax: +1 (602) 462 8801
Pittsburgh	Capgemini U.S. US Steel Tower 600 Grant Street, Suite 4780 Pittsburgh, PA 15219	Phone: +1 (412) 227 1100 Fax: +1 (412) 227 1101
San Francisco	Capgemini U.S. 555 California Street Suite 1800 San Francisco, CA 94104	Phone: +1 (415) 738 1300 Fax: +1 (415) 738 1301
Seattle	Capgemini U.S. 10500 NE 8th Street Suite 1400 Bellevue, WA 98004	Phone: +1 (425) 818 3300 Fax: +1 (425) 818 3301
Tampa	Capgemini U.S. 100 North Tampa Street, Suite 2350 Tampa, FL 33602-5197	Phone: +1 (813) 225 4747 Fax: +1 (813) 225 4847
Vienna (VA)	Capgemini U.S. 8000 Towers Crescent Drive Suite 800 Vienna, VA 22182	Phone: +1 (571) 382 6000 Fax: +1 (571) 382 6001
Westlake Village	Capgemini U.S. 31255 Cedar Valley Drive Suite 319 Westlake Village, CA 91362	Phone: +1 (818) 575 3500 Fax: +1 (818) 991 4606